Book to Movie

How to turn a book into a movie or TV series.

Scripts, Film Production, Funding, The Process, Obstacles and Legalities.

By

James Overtone

ALL RIGHTS RESERVED. This book contains material protected under International and Federal Copyright Laws and Treaties.

Any unauthorized reprint or use of this material is strictly prohibited. No part of this book may be reproduced or transmitted in any form or by any means, electronic, mechanical or otherwise, including photocopying or recording, or by any information storage and retrieval system without express written permission from the author.

Copyright © 2018

Published by: Zoodoo Publishing

Table of Contents

Table of Contents 3

General Introduction 6

SECTION ONE: THE FILMMAKING INDUSTRY 8

Chapter 1: Understanding the Movie Industry 9

A look at the Global Movie Industry 9

The Prospect of the Movie Industry 10

A Brief Look at Popular Movie Industries across the Globe 12

Hollywood 12

Difference between TV Series and Movies 15

Types of Movies 20

Types of TV Shows/Series 23

Chapter 2: Film Making 25

Myths about Filmmaking 25

Stages of Film Production 28

Various Companies Involved in Film Production/Film Production Crew 31

Chapter 3: Funding a Movie 36

Ways of Financing a Movie 36

Various Film Financing Models 38

Funding Sources for Various Countries 45

Companies Involved in Film Production Industry 58

SECTION TWO: FROM A BOOK TO A MOVIE 66

Chapter 4: The Process of Turning Your Book into a Movie 67

   Making Your Book Work First 67

   Turning Your Book into a Screenplay 68

   How to Get Your Screenplay Solicited 77

   Is It Right to Follow Up Your Submission? 78

   Pitching: An Important Aspect of a Query Letter 79

   Optioning Your Screenplay 80

   Do I Need to Get Attachment for My Movie? 84

   Production 86

   Royalty and Reselling Rights 87

   Creating a Book into a TV Series 88

   Storyrocket: A Useful Resource for Writers and Scriptwriters 89

SECTION THREE: THE LEGAL STUFF 91

Chapter 5: Copyright Protection Law 92

   Overview of the Copyright 92

   What Is Protected By Copyright Law 94

   Protecting Your Book/Screenplay 96

   What to Do When Your Right Is Infringed On 96

   Who Owns the Copyright: Producer Or the Author? 97

   Difference between Authorship and Ownership of Copyright 98

Chapter 6: Obstacles to Avoid 99

   Identifying and Dealing with all Right Transaction Pitfalls 99

   Get All the Rights from the Real Owners 99

   Know the Rights that Are Included in the Deal 100

Keep to Your Obligation to Avoid the Loss of Your Rights *100*

Be Mindful of Characters *100*

Getting Educated about the Movie Industry *101*

Chapter 7: Bonus **103**

Are There Directories For Books Made Into Movies? *103*

Are There Directories For Film Producers Of Specific Genres? *103*

What Are the Consequences of Adapting My Book Into a Movie Or TV Series? *104*

What Are Things You Should Not Bore Yourself With *105*

General Introduction

Adapting your book into a movie or a TV series is a veritable means of earning more money from your book. You will be paid by the movie producer that turns your book into a film. If the movie sells very well, you will also sell more of your book, as many people that watch the movie will look for the book. It will also increase your popularity as an author. Many authors nowadays are adapting their books into movies due to numerous benefits they obtain from such projects. According to the estimation of the author of *Film and/Is Art,* John Harrington, about one third to one fourth of all the movies produced globally are adapted from novels, short stories, classic literatures, plays, dramas and other literary forms. It is a reality that I have known right from the time I became of age. As a schoolchild, we read several classic literatures such as *Macbeth, Julius Caesar, The Merchant of Venice, Romeo and Juliet* and many more. These classic literary works of the great Shakespeare were all adapted into movies by different movie producers. The movies are also available in different languages. The same can also be said of literary works of other classical authors. Even modern authors and students of literature also have their works turned into movies or TV shows despite the fact that some people believe that printed texts are not only more moral but also superior to the film version. Thus, it is not a new thing for one to put a hot selling book into film. If you have a book that is already selling fast on the market or you are intending to write one, you can also consider turning it into movie or TV series in order to increase the revenue you make from your work.

The aim of this work is to guide you into adapting your book to a movie. The book also takes a look at the movie industry so as to enlighten newbies about the industry and provide them with insight into the various aspects of filmmaking. Among other things, it highlights the importance of copyright documentation. The book is limited in scope and thus does not cover everything about adaptation of a book to a movie. Given this, I advise that you also seek expert advice if you have a book that you will want to turn into a movie.

This publication is written from the view point of a person that has written and adapted a work into a movie. All the practical tips provided in the book are born out of practical experience. If you apply them as advised, they will be of help to you.

The book has three sections. The first section dwells on the movie industry. The objective of this section is to disclose the movie industry to you so that you will have a good understanding of what it is all about. The second section provides you with guidelines and instructions on what to do in order to create a film version of your book. You are going to find out from this section what it will take to begin and complete the project and what you stand to gain from it. The third section deals with the rights and other legal related topics in the movie industry. I wish you happy reading.

Important note: at the time of printing, all the websites mentioned in this book were working. As the internet changes rapidly, some sites might no longer be live when you read this book. That is, of course, out of our control.

SECTION ONE: THE FILMMAKING INDUSTRY

Turning your book into a movie implies moving from the literary world to another world. It is therefore essential that you have a clearer understanding of the industry, the prospect it has for you, various resources that will be of help to you, stakeholders in the industry and various aspects of the industry. Knowing the market will be of help to you to make certain decisions about your book. For example, you will be in a better position to decide whether to create a screenplay for TV series or movie from your book. Apart from that, you need to know the nature of the market you are entering. In this way, you will speak like a professional. Exposition of the important aspects of the market is the task I set to accomplish in this first section of the book. Take time to read it before moving to the next section that discusses practical steps.

Chapter 1: Understanding the Movie Industry

Who and what constitute the movie industry? Who are the major stakeholders in the industry? Does the industry include TV shows? What is the difference between movies and TV? How lucrative is the movie industry? Will you make a reasonable income from it? These are some of the questions that we are going to look into in this chapter of the book.

A look at the Global Movie Industry

As implicit from the name, the film industry is a part of entertainment industry that handles the production and distribution of movies. It also takes care of TV shows. The film industry is one that involves a lot of businesses and or individuals as there are different stages in the production of films. Each stage is handled by different professionals or businesses. Given the large number of people and businesses employed in the making of a movie either directly or indirectly, the motion picture industry plays an important role in the labour market of every country. Based on the same reason, it is also very expensive to produce a movie, as a lot of people will need to be paid.

Later in this book, I am going to discuss the various stakeholders in the industry. But suffice it to mention that the movie industry is a large one which consists of film producers, directors, actors and actresses, the film studios (theatre and cinema) film production, cinematography, film festivals, screenwriting, pre and post production activities, distribution and others. A lot of equipment and technology are also deployed in these businesses that take part in the production of movies. In other words, the industry has both technological and commercial aspects.

However, these actors don't have the same significance or are not of the same importance in the industry. The individuals or businesses that are considered the most influential in the industry, at least from the artistic view point, are the screenwriters and directors. The consumers or the man in the street may not know these people because they don't appear on the screen. The majority of the movie enthusiasts can recite litany of actors and actresses they know and the various movies and TV shows they have watched. But only a few can really tell who the directors and screenwriters of those movies are. In reality, behind the scenes, they put in more effort than any of participants in film creation as far as the visual techniques utilised and creation of a movie's storyline are concerned.

However, film directors and screenplay writers are of little consequence in matters relating to finance, marketing and all business aspects of movie creation. This is why they don't have much control over their own work from a business point of view. The film producers are the major players in this aspect. They are the financier and marketers of movies. They fund the production of a movie and also hire various people and businesses that will participate in the creation of a movie. The role or the extent of influence exercised by producers differs from one industry to another. There are some producers that only fund the production of a film. But there are some that will take up other functions. It is also possible to have multiple producers in a movie. In such a situation, only one or two of these producers will be actively involved in the production of the movie.

There are other people that play some roles that are not considered very significant. In most cases, the public knows nothing about these people. For example, there are some people that are employed simply to take care of certain personal needs of the actors and production crew. For example, during the shooting of a movie, some people are responsible for laundering and ironing the clothes of the actors and cleaning their rooms or rooms where action will take place. These people that offer these little and homely services normally receive little remuneration for their services when compared with the pay given to the other actors. Though, their functions are not highly regarded and remunerated in the industry, they make up a greater number of the participants in the industry when compared with the number of other personnel such as scriptwriters, producers, director, actors and others involved in a movie.

Generally speaking, the movie industry is a booming and lucrative industry. However, the economic advantage and prospects are not the same in all countries. Some countries are more popular than others when it comes to movie production and consumption of films by consumers. In other words, certain countries have a larger movie market than others making them to have a more profitable motion picture industry than others. Movies from such countries are exported to other parts of the world with a smaller film market. The movies are translated into the local language of the countries where they will be sold.

The Prospect of the Movie Industry

The movie industry is economically a vibrant one. It is an economy driving industry. The film entertainment is a big business in various part of the world including the North America, China, UK, Nigeria, India and others. For example, 14% of the US population go to cinema at least once a month, 31% go to movie a couple of times in year while another significant number that constitutes about 6% of the entire population of the country watch movies in the movie theatres at least two or three times in a month. The US alone has over 5,800 cinemas.

Generally speaking, the global filmmaking industry has a robust prospect. The global box office revenue of the industry in 2016 was US$38.6 billion. The projection in the coming years looks great. Experts believe that the global box office revenue of the film industry will increase to US$50 by 2020. As I already mentioned above, some countries are performing better than others in many aspects of this industry. India, Nigeria and the United States of America produce the largest number of movies than any other country. But in terms of revenue generation, United States, China, Japan, India and Great Britain have the largest markets by box office.

Given these differences, some places have become the headquarters of the movie industry. This means that most movies are produced in these places. In the United States of America, Hollywood California is the hub of movie production. Hong Kong is also a well known movie location for the Chinese movie industry. The major locations for film production in Europe are the United Kingdom, Spain, France, Italy and Germany.

These centres of film production are mainly the places where film producing industries are located. These places are different from the locations where the movies are shot. For some reasons, such as labour and infrastructure costs, some producers may decide to film their movies in a location different from where they are. For example, Nigeria has a large movie industry known as Nollywood but most of the Nigerian movies are shot in Ghana. Similarly, a lot of US movies are filmed in Canada. Indian movie producers also travel to places like Singapore, Europe and Americas to film their movies.

With the boom experienced and great prospect of the movie industry, participants in the movie industries including writers adapting their books to movies, screenwriters, producers, actors, directors and others are making a lot of money. For example, in 2014, the Hollywood's highest paid actor, Robert Downey JR earned $75 million.

There is no doubt that people may be wondering why the movie industry is still lucrative with a projection of many robust years ahead. Before now, there was fear that the motion picture industry will begin to experience some decline given the high cost of film production and the introduction of cable TV, digital piracy, VHS and TV. As I mentioned above, the number of people, individuals and families that go to movie theatres on a weekly, monthly and yearly basis is quite alarming. The operators of these cinemas make a lot of money from tickets sold out to these movie goers. Apart from these individuals going to cinema, filmmakers also make money from other derivative works such as home videos. TV series producers also make a lot of money via adverts that are shown intermittently during the show. Movie studios have also found other ways of making money with their production. Such of these film monetisation models include selling of overseas rights and pay-TV, amusement-park rides, creating tie-in video games and many others.

Note that success in film production is not a given, meaning that not all film making project turn out to be a success. Some producers have ended up with huge losses. For example, the producers of 47 Ronin ran a huge loss of $149.5 million. So, it is possible for things to go awry and your project will not yield any reasonable profit.

A Brief Look at Popular Movie Industries across the Globe

Hollywood
Hollywood is a popular name among movie enthusiasts. It is the name for the US movie industry. The industry has existed for over 121 years. Thus, it is the oldest cinema in the world and also the largest in terms of revenue generation. It has world class facilities and well equipped film studios such as the Lightstorm Entertainment, Metro-Goldwyn-Mayer, Paramount Pictures and 20th Century Fox. Hundred of movies are produced by these studios on a yearly basis not just for the American market but also for other countries' market. Examples of popular movies that were produced in Hollywood's studios are *Titanic, Avatar, Star Wars* and *Gone with the Wind*. The US Hollywood gross annual revenue between 2009 and 2015 was within the range of $10 billion and above. No other film industry in the world has made such gross annual revenue. The popular *The Oscars* is the Academy Awards of Hollywood normally hosted by the Academy of Motion Picture Arts and Science (AMPAS) on a yearly basis. Since the beginning of the ceremony, a total of 2,947 Oscars have been given out.

United Kingdom
The film industry in the United Kingdom has come of age and it is one of the most popular cinemas in the world. A number of high selling movies with huge box office returns such as James Bond and Harry Porter were produced in the UK. The industry also has produced a lot of actors with global acclamation and fame. Some of the internationally acclaimed actors

and Actress produced by the industry are Kate Winslet, Sean Connery, Michael Caine and Maggie Smith.

The UK movie industry has existed for over a century. However, the industry witnessed the most remarkable progress during the 1940s. This is the reason why some people consider these periods "the golden age" of the UK movie industry. This was the time of great directors like Michael Powell, David Lean and Carol Reed. The industry generates a lot of revenue for the Brits. The industry generated about $2 billion gross revenue in 2009 and obtained a global market share of 7%. With this figure, its market share in the UK was 17%.

Canada

The Canadian cinema or filmmaking industry boasts of a number of film studios with global acclamation. Some of these studios are located in Toronto, Montreal and Vancouver, which are regarded as the largest metropolitan centres in Canada. Canada's filmmaking industry reflects its regionalised political structure. The English speaking part of Canada has a stronger movie industry, which has produced about 1000 feature-length films while the cinema of the francophone part of the country has produced 6,000 feature-length films starting from 1911.

Though Canada has a unique cinema industry, her filmmaking industry has a strong link with that that of the US. As already mentioned above, Canada is the filming location of many US movies. A lot of US movie producers for one reason or the other film their movies in Canada. Given the healthy rapport between the country's cinema industries, there are some Canadian films that have American Identity and some American movies that have Canadian identity.

The filmmaking industry in Canada has produced a lot of actors some of whom (like Ryan Gosling, Norma Shearer, Mary Pickford, Jim Carrey and Donald Sutherland) have become prominent figures in Hollywood films. Well known filmmakers of the industry are James Cameron, Michael Snow, Allan King, Philippe Falardeau, Xavier Dolan, Lea Pool, Jean-Marc Vallee, Denis Villeneuve and others. The major Canadian distributors are Alliance Atlantis, Lions Gate Entertainment and others. The filmmaking industry in the country hosts a number of festivals which include the Toronto International Film Festival, Halifax, Vancouver International Film Festival, Atlantic Film Festival and other festivals held in other cities in Canada. The major distributors in the Canadian movie industry are Warner Bros, Universal and Disney.

China

The history of Chinese cinema dated back to 1896. The industry produced its first movie in 1905, which was titled *The Battle of Dingjunshan*. Hengdian World Studio of the Chinese movie industry is the largest film studio in the world. The centre of the movie industry in the country is Shanghai, which is the largest city in the Far East. Two of the movie and drama production complex and film studios in China, namely, the Oriental Movie Metropolis and Hengdian World Studio are the largest in the world. As of 2016, the Chinese movie industry has the largest number of screens, which was put at 44,179. The industry has continued to witness a significant growth generating US$6.58 billion in 2016 as its annual box office. It moved a step forward as the third largest film industry by number of feature films produced in 2010 to the second largest in 2012.

Today, China has become the centre of business for a lot of Hollywood studios. A lot of experts are projecting the Chinese movie industry to be the largest theatrical market by 2019. The major distributors of the industry are China Film, Huaxia and Enlight. Since 2016, 772 fictional movies, 49 animated films and 32 documentary movies have been produced in the industry. Some of the popular movies produced by the Chinese movie producers are Spring in a Small Town, Evening Rain, Hibiscus Town, Legend of Tianyun Mountain, One and Eight, Yellow Earth and many more.

India

The Indian movie industry is another popular movie industry in the world. The industry is second to Hollywood in terms of age. It has existed for more than a century. India remains unbeatable in the global industry in terms of the number of movies produced on a yearly basis. She has also edged every other country in the industry with her large number of admissions. Though, her movie industry is the 5th largest cinema in terms of revenue generated, it sells the highest number of tickets on a yearly basis. It should have been generating the largest revenue if not for its ticket price which is among the lowest in the world.

Cinema in India has remained unique and has continued to increase in popularity because it is multilingual. India has a number of film industries unlike many countries that have only one or two. The largest movie industry in the country is known as Bollywood. It accounts for 20% of all the movies produced in India. Other big movie industries that make significant contribution in the growth of the country's movie industries are Bangla Cinema (the Cinema of West Bengal known as Tollywood), Tamil Cinema (referred to as Kollywood), Telugu cinema (Tollywood), Kannada cinema (Sandalwood), Malayalam cinema (Mollywood) and others. These industries are also located in different parts of the country. The major movie locations in India are Chennai, Hyderabad, Bengaluru, Kochi and Kolkata. Indian movies, especially Bollywood movies, are growing in popularity across the world. Movies made in these film industries are watched in various parts of the world such as Australia, Europe, New Zealand, Nigeria, Ghana, South Asian countries, Gulf countries and other countries. Ramoji Film City which situates in Hyderabad, India is the largest film studio complex in the world.

Africa

Egypt and Nigeria have the most popular movie industries in Africa. The centre of movie production in Egypt where majority of Egyptian movies and TV series are made is the Egyptian Media Production City. The facility has equipment for both indoor and outdoor shooting. The Egyptian cinema has remained on top in the Middle East even though, it is faced with a number of obstacles. The Nigerian movie industry on the other hand is known as the Nollywood. It is second to the Indian movie industry when it comes to the number of movies produced on a yearly basis. It generates the third largest income when compared with other movie industries in the world. Nollywood has produced actors and actress with global acclamation such as Kenneth Okonkwo, Ramsey Nouah, Omotola Jalade Ekehinde, Ini Edo, Bob-Manuel Udokwu, Genevieve Nnaji and others.

With this discussion on various movie industries, I believe by now, you will know what the industry looks like and some of the countries with the best market. In the foregoing discussion, I have been mentioning movies, films, cinema, TV shows/series and in some instances using the terms interchangeable. These words are very similar but they don't have the same meaning in all circumstances. In the subsequent subtitle, I will discuss them so that you will know how they differentiate from each other.

Difference between TV Series and Movies

TV series and movies are important elements of the film or cinema industry. Each of these aspects of the entertainment industry has fans. There are also producers and actors that specialise in them and have amassed wealth for themselves through them. In the TV series, which is also known as soap operas, we hear of popular actors and actresses like the UK Lesley Saweard, the Australian Ray Meagher, the US Eileen Fulton and many others. These TV series actors have become as popular as their counterparts in the movie industries. The essence of these two aspects of the film industry is to entertain the viewers. However, in reality, there are some differences between them. If you want to adapt your book into a movie, it is of crucial importance that you know the difference between the two so that you will know which one will suit your work (note that it is a producer that will decide that). I am going to explain the difference between these two aspects of film show. I will also discuss other similar words like cinema, theatre and film.

What is a movie?

A movie refers to recorded moving pictures and sounds that narrate a story, which may be fictitious or real, shown in a movie theatre or a cinema. A movie is a form of entertainment and therefore, its major essence is to entertain the viewers. The pictures and sounds can also be displayed to educate or pass important information to the viewers. Regardless of the reason why a movie is being produced and shown to enthusiasts, the maker has an aim in mind which is to bring the enthusiasts to the movie theatre or make them purchase other derivatives works such DVDs of the movie so that they will make money from it. It requires a lot of money to shoot a movie. A lot of tools and equipment are also used. The term movie sometimes can be used synonymously with film. But as I will show below, there are also some nuances as the words evolve overtime.

What is a TV series?

TV series are very much similar to movies in production and nature. They are motion pictures recorded with sounds that are broadcast or aired through cable television or Internet television. But unlike movies, the aim for which they are aired to the viewers is for commercial purposes and not just to entertain the viewers. The makers make their money through these adverts that are shown when the program is being aired. The advertisers pay for the times their products are televised during the program. But from the viewers' point of view, they watch the program in order to get entertained or learn something. Another defining aspect of a TV series is that it is shown through a cable television or online television and not in a cinema or movie theatre.

The table below shows the major difference between these two aspects of the film industry.

Movie	TV series
The display is not interrupted by adverts as it is not commercialised (note that today, producers are also using their movies to market a product in a number of ways; but the major difference is that viewing experience is not interrupted by adverts).	The program shown is commercialised. Consequently, adverts are intermittently put up during the show and this can sometimes interrupts the users' viewing experience, which can be annoying. But this is a welcome development for the sponsors. TV series are therefore sponsored programs for the purposes of popularising the sponsor's brand, products and services.
Movies are reflection of creative talent. Their makers can try different concepts which necessarily do not based on what is in vogue	TV series on the other hand are majorly based on a concept that is correctly in vogue.
Movies are capital intensive, meaning that a lot of money is required to produce them. Besides, the production of movies can be carried out within various environments, indoors and outdoors. They require various kinds of equipment.	TV series are also expensive to make but they are not as expensive as movies. Most soap operas are produced in an indoor environment or just in an indoor theatre (there are a few that can be produced in an outdoor environment).
Movies normally take a shorter duration to be completed. Most of them usually last between the range of 1.5 hour and 3 hours.	Soap opera has a longer duration. The duration varies. But in general, they are normally lengthy programs consisting of many episodes. There are some that may last for months or more than a year.

Movie	TV series
Movies differ from TV series in the medium in which they are shot. They are shot in 70mm.	TV series on the other hand are shot in 35 mm (note that this difference does not affect the viewers' experience of TV series as they also enjoy the show just as movie viewers do.
Movies do not have as wide reach as TV series. Only people that go to cinema or purchase the film can see it.	TV series have wider reach.

Cinema and Movies: How Synonymous Are They?

Movie and cinema as well as other words like show, theatre and flick have similar meaning that people sometimes use them interchangeably. In certain circumstances, they can mean the same thing. But there are still some nuances between them. It will also be good that you know the circumstances under which they differ.

People normally watch movies as a means of relaxing themselves and getting entertained and having some fun during their free time. When people watch them, they laugh and forget about their problems. It can also awaken their feelings and make them cry. It is also a good way of showcasing a persons way of life. As explained above, it is a type of motion picture recorded with sound. It tells and plays the story contained in the screenplay written by a screenwriter. The story can be adapted from a book or written directly by a scriptwriter.

The term movie can be used also to refer to a film. People normally use the world movie as an informal expression for a film. It can also be used to mean the facility where a film is shown to fans or enthusiasts. In this regard, it can have the same meaning with a cinema or a movie theatre. The word also means motion picture displayed in cinema for commercial or public viewing. It can also mean home-made videos.

Cinema under certain circumstances can have the same meaning as a movie. For example, it can mean a facility where films or motion images are shown to the public. One can say that they are going to the cinema or movies. Cinema also refers to the medium through which recorded motion pictures are displayed on screen. In this connotation, it is a device for projecting films on a screen or another suitable medium. The word in this regard is French in origin. It was invented in the 19th century. At the initial time, it was used to record day-to-day activities such as shopping. Later, it was used to record scripted stories. As cinema evolved, it gained different meanings. It can now be used to mean the entire art and process of movie, the medium for displaying a movie, a theatre for exhibition of shows, plays, films and movies. Take a look at the table below to see how the word cinema compares with movie.

Movie	Cinema
It is used to refer to commercial cinema shown to large audience with the objective of making gain from it.	The word can be used to stand for a theatre or facility for showing of films. It also refers to the entire movie industry.
Movie is an art of creating moving images and pictures recorded with sounds.	Cinema can be taken to be the art form of the cinema industry.
Movie can also refer to the process through which films are made.	Cinema on the other hand is based on filmmaking or movie making process as well as the process of editing, designing and scriptwriting it.
It has various types or genres which include comedy, horror, thriller, action, detective movies etc.	There are also various kinds of cinema industries across the world such as Hollywood, Bollywood, Nollywood, British Cinema, the Filmmaking Industry of Canada, French cinema and others.

Video and Film

Video and film are popular words in the movie industry also used interchangeably by many people. Under certain circumstances, they can have the same meaning but there are subtle differences between them. Here are the various ways they differ from each other.

Video	Film
Video refers to motion pictures recorded on VHS, cassette, VCD, DVD or in any other suitable format.	Film is a type of moving pictures and recorded but not meant to be displayed to the public or commercialise like a cinema.
A video can be described as a cold medium as a result of its clinical life's interpretation.	A film is regarded as a warm medium because of the effects it has on human eyes. The frame lines as well as hairs and dust are quickly projected making it difficult for the eyes to see but their presence can be felt by the mind.
Video data are available in digital and tape format and thus, they can easily be copied to a computer.	Editing of films can be accomplished physically by cutting and taping. It is also possible to digitize it into a computer.
A video operates at the rate of 24 frames per second.	Film moves at the rate of 25 frames per second.
Its resolution is low.	Its resolution is high.
It has harsh quality.	Its quality is high.

Types of Movies

Just as we have various kinds of literary works, movies are available in different types. If you are planning to adapt your book to a movie, it is essential that you know the various kinds of movies and their meaning. Knowing them will help you to determine the type that will suit your book most. Here are the various kinds of movies.

Action movies
These types of movies are exactly as they sound. They are full of action, showing violent scenes like chases, stunts, wars, fights, battles, destruction with weapons etc. Depending on the movie, different kinds of weapons of warfare such as guns, tanks, jet fighters, war helicopters, swords, horses, cars and the likes are being utilised. The battle is also between one city and

the other or between the forces of bad guys. In some of these types of movie, the good guys always triumph over the bad ones. There are also some of them where good guys do have a tragic end. The kind of weapons to use depends on the nature of the story being told. It can be swords and spears. It can also be AK 47, tanks, war jets and many more. Martial arts films also come under this classification.

Adventure films
It is a movie that narrates the story of an event. It can be about an exploration into an unknown, a voyage, a journey into an unfamiliar location and the likes. Searches, historical spectacles, disaster films, treasure hunts and the likes are also included in this kind of movie.

Dramas
Drama is an important part of literature. Normally, dramas are meant to tell a story which may be real or derived from real life events. They have a strong plot. Such movies also have real settings. They are not fictitious or based on scientific fiction. Dramas are of different types and they together constitute the largest genre of movies.

Epic/historical movie
It is a kind of classical movie that tells the story of historic event or a legendary figure. The story may have root on mythology even though the setting and plot may be presented to be real. The costumes used in acting such movies are normally expensive and they are classical in style and design. Biblical films or Greek mythological movies like Hercules are typical examples of such a movie.

Comedy
Comedy is a story with a happy ending plotted to amuse the audience. The plots or storyline may be an imagined or factual situation. It can also be built around people's daily routine and lifestyle under an environment such as family, workplace, school, and the likes. But the essence is to make the audience laugh and forget about their worries. The actors normally achieve this via the languages they use, crude jokes, facial expression, exaggerations and the like.

Crime and gangster films
These kinds of movies really mean what they sound like. They are films that showcase the activities or operations of gangsters or criminals. The storyline can be drawn from a real life situation. It can also be imagined. Movies about terrorism, bank robbery, serial killers and the likes are typical examples of crime and gangster film genres.

Horror film
This kind of film is made to cause fear or terrify the viewers. The plots are made to frighten and shock the viewers but in a unique manner. The viewers are frightened by the plots but at the same time, they are entertained. Most parents will not want their children to view such movies as some of them will be frightened to the extent of crying when the movie is being shown. It may also make them have nightmares and develop phobias of their rooms when it is dark. Horror film scriptwriters nowadays incorporate science fiction and fantasies into them. It can also be about zombies and vampires. Serial killers, terrorist activities, wizardry, cultists and occult operations can also be classified under this category. Thus, horror movies have various sub-genres.

Musical/ dance movies
These kinds of films incorporate music, song and dance in a unique manner in their storyline. Musical performance is an important aspect of the movie narrative. They are good movies for musical buffs. The famous *Sound of the Music* is a typical example of such a film.

Science fiction movies
Scientific fiction movies dwell on scientific and technological inventions. The plot may be real or just about futuristic technology. It can also be based on scientific fantasies, planetary and spatial realities and unusual monsters that resulted from mistakes of the scientists (or even created intentionally by miscreants among scientists). Science fiction movies resemble fantasy, adventure and action movies in certain aspects. There are some that incorporate some aspects of horror in it.

War films
These movies are made to replicate war situations in motion pictures. They can be used to show the real effect and devastating nature of war. Some war films can also be helpful to the military as they can be used to show and teach strategies of planning and executing military campaigns. The storyline can be to show a soldier's heroic act or their love for their fatherland and readiness to defend against any form of external aggression and invasion. Real weapons of warfare such as guns, tanks, bombs, swords, spears, and others are used for the battle in these movies. Some of them are classic and historical in nature while some have a contemporary setting. It is the setting that will determine the nature of the combat and the type of weapon that will be used. If the setting is classic in nature, then classic weapons like spears, horses, shields and swords are used.

Romantic and love movies

These movies are all about the story of love affairs and romance between two or more people. Some of such movies may have some adult contents or contents that may be considered too strong for minors or obscene in certain religious cycles. There are also some that are about love but do not contain any adult content. The screenplays of some of such movies are written with strong adult language that may be considered damaging to young people or aimed at arousing erotic feelings in the viewers. The producer determines the age for which it is meant. They are normally shown in adult cinema and viewers are most often warned of the possible sex scenes in the video if they contain any.

Westerns
This genre of movies is common in the American movie industry. They are meant to show how the American society gradually expanded and developed. The striking and unique aspects of these genres of movies are their characters, plots, and elements. Normally, their setting is that of the medieval period. Horses and six-gun as well as swords are the major weapons of warfare used in them. Their characters also include cowboys, Indians, dusty towns, and trails. The westerns as a genre of movie can be quite interesting to watch. It will appeal to people that have interest in classic movies.

Types of TV Shows/Series

TV series and shows are very much similar to movies. But unlike movies, they are kinds of commercialised programs and shows aired over cable TV and Internet TV with the intention of entertaining the viewers and also popularising brand, product and services of the sponsors. Here are some of the kinds of TV programs or shows that you should know.

A costume drama: It is a kind of drama with a historical or classic setting.

A wildlife programme: In this kind of program, the lives of various kinds of animals in their natural habitat is televised. Popular animals that are shown are the big cat families, elephants, bears, hyenas, wolfs and anacondas and other kinds of wildlife.

A reality show: This type of program brings talented individuals together for a show of skills. Each reality show has the desired talent being sought for or the purpose for which the participants are assembled. The participants are assessed as they accomplish the tasks assigned to them.

Documentary shows: These are shows meant to enlighten the viewers on a particular subject matter. The content of such films does not have fictitious material inside. It is all based on facts and reality.

A docudrama: It is a type of film with a storyline based on real facts and events. As the name shows, it combines the elements of documentary and drama shows. To a certain extent, the actors replicate documented events. It also shows real events in a way. Such a TV programme will appeal to you, if you have interest in drama or documentary movies or both.

TV series: It is a term used to refer to a film or program which comprises several episodes aired on television or Internet television in regular intervals. The episodes are connected as they all deal with the same subject matter or they are a continuum.

Serial shows: It is similar to a series except that the show does not have a specified end and it is normally published in instalments.

Thriller: It is a kind of sensational film that keeps the viewers in suspense as they watch.

There are other kinds of TV shows meant for entertainment and enlightenment that are outside the scope of our discussion. Such categories are current affairs programmes, news programmes, game show, quiz shows and many others. All these kinds of TV shows and movies are also available in literature. It is the type of book that you have that will determine the kinds of screenplay that you will develop for your book. If you have not written any books yet, but you have a plan of writing one, you should go into the area that you have interest in. If you choose an area that you are passionate about, you will definitely do it very well.

Chapter 2: Film Making

The preceding chapter provides an insight into the industry defining and differentiating similar terminologies such as movies, films, cinema and TV shows. It also discusses the popular movie industries across the globe and the various kinds of movies and TV shows all with the sole intention of helping you to understand the industry. Now, it is time to discuss the filmmaking process to enable you to know the various process your book will undergo in order to come out as a movie if it is eventually green lighted by a producer to be made into a movie or TV show. The various businesses and individuals that are involved in the movie making industries are also explained in this book. I am going to start this chapter by exposing and debunking some of the myths about the filmmaking process and filmmaking industries.

Myths about Filmmaking

A lot has been said about filmmaking processes and the cinema industry in general. If you ask Google any question about the movie making industry, there is no doubt that you will get a lot of answers, some of which may be contradictory. Thus, it is essential that you have the right information about the industry that you are trying to enter into. This will be of help to you as, with the right information, you will be talking like a professional. Below are some myths about this industry that you be aware of.

1. People with talents are the most successful in the movie industry.

Some people believe that one needs to be very skilful and talented in order to be successful in the movie industry. This may be partly correct and partly false depending on the angle you are looking at. It is true, if you are viewing it from the point that it is almost impossible to be successful in anything if you lack the basic theoretical and practical skills required in the field. However, if you look at it from business and profit aspect of it, the talented people in the industry don't get the full benefits of their skills and effort. They receive only a peanut compared to what those with the business and financial power make. Put differently, it is those that understand the business aspects of movie making that excel higher than others. This does not mean that talent is not required to succeed in the industry. Even if you understand the commercial aspects of movie making, you still require some basic business skills in order to be successful in the industry. The implication of this is that to be successful in the movie industry and to reap the fruit of your labour, it is of crucial importance that you have a good understanding of the commercial aspects of the business. Know how to make negotiations and bargain for the most favourable terms and conditions when selling your book.

2. Only the best script can be filmed and produced.

Some people have good books or even well written screenplay and yet it is not made or taken up during pitching. There are a number of factors that may contribute to that. The major point that you should bear in mind here is that regardless of how articulated, professional and well written your script or book is, it will not get made if your book is not solicited by any producer or agent meaning that nobody is willing to finance the adaptation into a movie. Experience has shown that producers or financiers sometimes as a result of human weakness solicited and sponsored a wrong book or script. The trick to getting your script made into a movie is to know how to get solicited and develop an appealing business plan which a financier cannot reject. This is why I say in the first myth that people who succeed are those that have a good knowledge of the business aspect of it.

3. Filmmaking is capital intensive.

It is a commonly accepted belief that filmmaking requires huge capital. This may be true but it is not always the case. There are a number of movies that are produced with little amount of money. If you have attended or watched Raindance Film Festival program on television, you will definitely noticed that there are a number movies shown there that were not costly. It all depends on the type of movies, the setting and locations where it is produced as well as the equipment used in producing it. There is what is known today as micro budget film. If you are going into the movie industry with little budget, it is essential that you take time to learn what it means and how it is achieved. You can take your time to see some of these inexpensive films of the festivals on Raindance VoD channel if you are living in the UK.

4. You must have a degree in filmmaking before you can make films.

Many people believe that one who does not have a degree or does not attend any filmmaking programme of studies cannot be a producer. This is far from the truth. It is like saying that one has to complete a study programme in literature or a related course before they will be able to write a book of any type. There are many literary luminaries that do not specialise in literature and yet they were able to write great novels, poems, drama, prose and different kinds of books. In a similar, there are many successful movie makers as well as actors that have no degree in filmmaking. You can still create a wonderful movie even if you have no degree in the field. All you need is to have the interest and also to make time to study the industry, business aspect of it, watch movies to learn the language used in the industry. Once you are familiar with the industry, you can excel. However, this does not mean that it is not necessary to enrol in a movie program in a film school. If you have the time and money, you can also attend a movie school. You can learn a lot from movie schools and also increase your contact. But bear in mind that there are a lot of things that you will not learn in the filmmaking industry. If you take a look at the list of participants in the last year's Sundance Film Festival, you will be surprised at the number of them that attended filmmaking schools.

5. You must have an agent to progress in the movie industry.

The cinema industries have a number of agents that help actors, producers, screenwriters, directors and other participants in the industry in one way or the other. Given the various roles discharged by these agents, many people believe one needs an agent to get involved in the industry. This is not true. You can also do things for yourself. For example, you don't need any agent to get an acting role if you are interested in acting. You don't need any person to do any negotiation on your behalf when you want to sell your script. Agents are middlemen. Their roles are very important in case you cannot carry out the service they are doing creditably well. In this case, if you don't know the business side of the movie industry very well or if you are not able to negotiate favourable terms for yourself, you can hire an agent to do it for. But you are going to pay for their services.

6. Digital shooting is cheaper than filming.

Digital shooting is an affordable means of producing a movie. However, it is not always the case. It all depends on the type of movie you want to produce, your budget and circumstances. So, before you decide on whether to do digital shooting or filming, you need to contact your lab and obtain quotes. From the quotes, you will have an idea of which option is the best.

7. Filmmakers do not require social media.

Many people have bought into the idea that filmmakers do not need social media in order to become popular in the industry and promote their work. No! You need social media to sell your movie. Festival programmers and acquisition executives are interested in filmmakers that have great social media profiles with a large number of followers. Some of the Festival programmers pay for movies simply because of the social media strategy of the filmmakers. Oren Pelli is a typical example of a filmmaker that sold his movie because of his social media strategy. Paramount purchased his Paranormal Activity simply because of his successful social media strategy. So, you need to be a good social media communicator; learn how to go after interesting profiles on the Internet. You should strive towards building a large circle of followers.

8. You need to bring in a large number of people on debut/premiere. The number of people that are present during your red carpet premiere does not actually matter or determine how quick you will sell your work. You don't actually need to have many people at your premiere. Only a few individuals are important and they include the buyers of the movies, people that take decisions regarding which movies are selected, those that decide what are aired via TV and the people that determine which films that are selected and programmed at the film festivals. You should do everything to get these people to see your movie. Veritable avenues of getting these people see your movies are via trailers and press kit posters. It is essential that you have good understanding of how to create and utilise these channels very well.

There may be other myths about film production. These are just the most common ones. I shall also expose and puncture myths about screenplay writing in the chapter where it is treated. You can also look for other myths. It is difficult to avoid coming across these myths on the Internet as many people intentionally post unfounded stories. So, you need to carry out thorough research in order to know and learn the right thing.

Stages of Film Production

Having examined the various myths about movie production, it is now time to talk about the various stages of film production. Filmmaking or the production of movies goes through several stages before the final products get to the consumers. There are 7 basic stages in the process of movie production. It is also important that you know these stages. You may be wondering why it is important that you know the various stages of film production since you can sell your book to a producer who will handle every other process. Planning to turn your book into a movie implies that you are entering into the movie industry, which requires that you know everything about the industry. That is what it means to be a professional in the industry. So, you can see why it is important that you learn about it. Here are the various stages of the film making process.

Development stage

The first step in the production of most movies is the creation of a script or the screenplay or story outline. The script can be adapted from an already existing book or it can be written afresh. This stage can also start from the pitching of an idea to a producer. So, where the development starts depends on the project or the film in question. Regardless of where it starts, the development stage is a very crucial stage as the success of the movie depends on it. It is the foundation upon which the remaining stages are built. For example, you cannot produce any movie without a script. If you have a well-written script and you did not succeed during the pitching, producers will not accept to fund the production of the movie. So, it is therefore of crucial importance that you write it very well.

Pre-production

The second phase in the production of a film is the pre-production phase. In this phase, filmmakers make their production choices and go for what is necessary or what can meet their budget. This stage can be referred to as the planning stage because it is during this stage that all plans about the movie are made before filming takes place. Things that are planned in this stage include making the choice of location for the shooting of the movie. The constitution of the production crew is also decided during this stage. The producer will hire a production or line manager to work with. The budget for the production of the movie is made at this stage. Every arrangement and schedule is made at this period.

Production

This is the phase where the production of the movie is planned before the daily shooting. It is different from the preproduction stage as it concerns the arrangement for the daily shooting or filming of the movies. The budget and all schedules have been made during the pre-production stage. During this stage, effort should be made to keep to them. If you fail to keep to the budget for example, you may have some financial difficulties along the line. So, you need to be alert and careful with the execution of the project so that you will not go beyond budget. Another important skill (if you like, call it a virtue) that should be highlighted in this stage is communication. It is essential that communication be maintained. All parties involved in the production of a movie should be properly updated especially on crucial issues like location, office, set, distributors, production company and others.

The rolling of the camera

This phase is the stage of principal photography. Every arrangement has been completed before now. It is now time for the camera to roll. This stage is capital intensive and the most expensive of all the phases. It is during this stage that most members (if not all) of the production crew including the actors, directors, cast directors, costume designer, production sound mixer and others get paid or part of their payment for services rendered. The number of people to be included in the film crew depends on the type of movie being produced and the budget of the producer.

Independent producers who are on a budget normally have a production crew made up of few people numbering about 8 to 9. However, in large movie industries, the film crew can be more than a hundred people. It is an important phase because all that were carried out in the other three phases above were done to ensure that this stage of principal photography goes smoothly, effectively and efficiently. Again, communication is very important in this phase. The production crew should also ensure that they work according to budget and schedule. It is also of crucial important for production to keep a complete record.

Wrapping up stage

The wrapping up stage comes immediately after the filming process. It overlaps with the principal photography stage. In this stage, the production crew put the stage, location and everything they use for production of the movie in order or as they are before they utilise them for the shooting. All hired equipment or tools should be returned to the supplier and all records maintained for reference purposes.

The production stage involves a lot of people and thus, there is a need for team spirit or concerted effort. It is not something that one person will achieve even though some people assume or play more crucial role. The number of hours it will take for the shooting to be completed depends on the casting location. At the end completion of the movie, most producers normally organise a wrap party in order to appreciate all people that were involved in the creation of the movie for their contribution towards the success of the movie.

Post-production

This is the second to the last stage in movie production. The stage brings the principal photography to an end. It may also overlap with the preceding stage. The major tasks carried out during this stage include assembling the movie, assessing the footage and all other editing works. The sound designs, music and visual effects are evaluated during this stage and necessary contributions made. After all contributions and editing have been carried out, the picture will be locked for the delivery elements to be made. This is an important stage as it is during this stage that all corrections are made before the final work is brought out. The major player in this phase is the video/film editor who will assemble the film and do all editing including the editing of the production sound. It is also during this phase that songs are composed; the design and recording of sound of effects also are carried out during this stage.

Distribution

The distribution stage is the last stage. This is the stage the movie is made available to the consumers. It is displayed in the movie theatres and at the cinema for the viewing consumers. Some producers also make their movies available online in various marketplaces such as Amazon for direct download for people that prefer using soft copy or the Internet.

This phase also involves promotion and marketing. Various advertising methods such as posters, press kits and others are used to popularise a movie product. During the launching of the movies, a number of activities can be organised. Such activities include a red carpet premiere, launch party, press preview screenings, interview with the press, press releases and film festival screenings. This phase of movie production is handled by a different company, the distribution company. The film's marketed and promoted in some cases through a special website different from the website of the producers or distributor. Promotion tours are also organised.

Various Companies Involved in Film Production/Film Production Crew

As I explained above, films are not made by one person. The production process involves a lot of people with each person or business carrying out a specific task. The number of people or businesses that participate in the production of movie is not a given. It all depends on the movie industries. Some independent movie producers work with a film crew that comprises a few people. But large cinema industries produce movies with a film crew that consists of a large number of people with each performing certain specific tasks. The crew of some industries for certain kinds of project can be up to or more than 100 people. If you are planning to adapt your book to a film, it is of crucial importance that you know the various individuals and businesses that will be involved in the project. The film crew is normally hired by the production company. Therefore, it is the producer of a movie that will determine the constitution of the film crew or the various departments that will be involved in the production of the movie. Each department or individual is assigned with a specific task. Here are some important members of a film crew.

Production departments

The film producer is one of the major persons involved in the production of a movie. He or she performs a lot of functions that are crucial for the success of the project. It is the producer that hires and pays other members of the crew. It could be said that other members of the crew are working for him or her. Production has different aspects and therefore apart from the film producer, there are other individuals that manage various aspects of production. So, we have various kinds of production managers including the following.

Unit production manager has the responsibility of handling the budget and schedule of the production. It also is their role to keep the financiers of the film and the studio executives posted on the progress of the project.
Location manager chooses the location for the shooting of the movie. It is also their responsibility to take care of the locations.

Executive producer (EP) previously handled the financial aspects of movie making and also played the creative role. But today, the function of the executive producer is somewhat confusing as it overlaps with the function of the initiating producer in some movie industries. It is therefore not uncommon for the line producer to play the role of the executive producer especially in the feature movies. In some movie projects, the executive producer can also discharge the function of the initiating producer. So, in the movie industry of today, the two offices interplay. Each plays the role of the other making it difficult for their job specification to be defined.

Line producer plays the function of a middleman between the studio and the production manager. He also ensures that movie production goes according to budget. As the name suggests, the office takes the responsibility of gathering and sourcing for resources required for the production of the movie.

Costume designer determines and chooses the costume or clothing for the actors and all the characters in the movie. They work in collaboration with the actors and closely with other departments. They may make decisions that will affect every member of the crew.

The makeup and hair designer is the person that makes up the actors and actresses to create the look required for a particular role. They also work in collaboration with the costume designer. In some projects, one person can handle or discharge the role of the costume designers and makeup and hair designer.

Director of photography handles and controls any function that is linked with the photography in any manner.

Casting director is in charge of the audition and shooting of the movie. He looks for the actors that will perform the various tasks and characters in the book.

Production sound mixer oversees the activities of the sound department during the production stage of the movie. They discharge their duties in collaboration with the boom operator, First AD, Director and DP and DA. It is their function to record and mix the audio on set.

Sound designer works with the supervising sound editor to develop the aural conception of the film. The office of the sound designer in certain cinema industries like Bollywood discharges the duties of the director of audiography which in some other filmmaking industries is a separate office.

Music composer begins their duty during the post production period. Their role is to compose new music for the film.

Production assistant, abbreviated as PA, works help the production office and other offices in discharging their duties. They carry out multiple tasks of general nature for other departments.

Assistant production manager helps the production manager to discharge his duties. Not all production managers have an assistant. It all depends on the movie that is being made. Normally, they are utilised in feature films with big budgets.

Production coordinator organises all logistics of production including renting of equipment, hiring the crew, booking for accommodation and places for the shooting of the movies and other similar tasks. His duty may interplay with some other functions but the office is very crucial to the production of movies.

Unit manager has a role that interplays or that is same with that of the production manager during secondary unit shooting. The function of the unit manager can also be handled by the transport coordinator in certain functional structures.

Assistant directors (AD) handle different offices with each office handling different tasks. There is the office of the first assistant director which helps the director and the production manager in the execution of their tasks. It is the function of the office of the AD to ensure the schedule is maintained. He also provides a suitable working environment for the director and other departments to discharge their duties creditably. The second assistant director assists the AD in carrying his tasks such as booking, scheduling and others. He also prepares the call sheet for the members of the crew so that everybody will know what to do and when to do it. He ensures that the crew members are kept posted with the detailed information about each of the shooting days. There are other assistant directors with defined functions such as the 3rd AD, 2nd AD and others. It all depends on the movie industries in question. Not all film productions require their services.

Accounting department
The accounting department is comprised of different personnel or offices. There is the production accountant who takes care of the production money and pays all the members of the crew and also ensures that everyone gets paid. The clerk, also referred to as the assistant accountant, handles the accounts payable, payroll and accounts receivable for the office of the production accountants.

Location scout has the responsibility of finding suitable possible locations for the shooting of a film. The responsibilities can also be handled by the location manager or assistant location manager for movies made on a budget.

Note that there are other people that help the location manager in handling matters relating to locations. They include the location assistant manager and location production assistant.

Legal counsels take care of the legal issues of film production. For example, they help the parties involved in negotiating favourable terms in any contract. It is the legal departments that also handle immigration paperwork, get tax credits from the local government authorities and also handles all rights issues involved in the films. They examine all contracts and approaches to ensure no law is violated or the producer will not have any legal battle with any person.

System administrator is an important person in the production of movies. He is employed to handle all computer related tasks including any network utilised during the production of movies. The system administrator is normally needed for digital intermediate editing. They also handle the digital monitors on set, digital sound and digital effects.

Casting director is responsible for the casting of the movie. It is the office of the casting director that selects actors and assigns roles to them. He invites the possible actors for a film and chooses those that he considers fit for various characters in the movie. In some projects, the cast director is given an assistant referred to as a cast personal assistant. The cast PA handles all requests both private and technical from actors.

Camera operator is an important person in the production of a movie even though they may not be put on a high profile. It is a camera operator that films the scenes during the casting. The quality of the production depends on his expertise to a certain extent. He follows the instruction and directives of the director of photography when taking shots and capturing scenes during shooting.

Director of photography is the highest person of the camera and lighting crew members. He works in collaboration with the film director in taking important decisions about the lighting and framing of the scenes. He chooses the right lens, lighting, composition and filter according to the instructions and requirements of the film director. The director of photography is also referred to as cinematographer in some movies. He is assisted by first assistant camera and second assistant camera.

There are other members of the crew or departments involved in filmmaking such as film loader, camera production assistant, digital imaging technician, steadicam operator and many more. As mentioned above, there are a number of factors such as the budget, the nature of the movie and the cinema industry that will determine the size or constitution of the film crew.

Now that we have learnt the various individuals and departments that handle different stages of the filmmaking process, it is now time for me to discuss the money involved in filmmaking and how to source funds for such a project.

Chapter 3: Funding a Movie

Many film students and authors that want to adapt their books into movies are seeking for advice on how they can finance such a project. Though nowadays there are budget friendly means of funding a filmmaking project, the making of a movie is always expensive. By this I mean that it is not something that you can easily finance with your savings unless you are a high earner or you have a large amount of savings. Even if you are using your iPhone to do the shooting, you will still have to spend some money in one way or the other as we will see later in the next section that talks about the film making process. Ask those who are into the filmmaking industry or who have shot a movie before, they will tell you that the gear and camera budgets are just a small fraction of the total budget. So, the truth is that you will face the reality of sourcing funds no matter how you want to approach the project. This is why I consider it pertinent to discuss this chapter.

Ways of Financing a Movie

One of the commonly and frequently asked questions by authors that will want to adapt their books into films or by newbies in filmmaking industries is 'who funds a filmmaking project'? Many articles have been written on that. Some of these articles mention funding sources like friends and relatives, banks and personal savings. Indeed, it is not always easy to obtain funding from some of these sources mentioned. If you are relying on a bank for example, you will still have to provide collateral to the bank before you are provided with sufficient funding. Besides, there are some other aspects of the process of obtaining loans from the bank that you may not be comfortable with. Most banks will take a look at your credit scores and may require some difficult-to-complete paperwork. In summary, it is indeed not easy to access loans from a bank. So, don't think that if you apply for a loan for the production of a movie, your bank will easily provide that to you. Even if you plan to use crowdfunding, it is also not easy to get investors to stake their money on the project. Many investors can only put money on a project that they are certain that will give them good return on investment. It is also very difficult to rely on friends and relatives for such a project. First, they may not have the required amount. Secondly, some of them may not be willing to give out their money. They may even discourage them for making such an attempt.

Many investors and funding sources are always reluctant to provide funds for the production of movies because they are not sure of the possibility of getting back their money. The factor they consider first is how much they will make from the movie if it is eventually made. They don't consider much about the cost of producing the movie but the profit it will bring. The implication of this is that if your movie is good and it is much likely that it will yield good return, it will be easier for you to obtain funding from various sources because your project has a high return on investment.

However, they remain veritable means of sourcing funds for the production of movies. But I am talking about their ugly sides or the difficulty involved in accessing funds through various funding source first in this discussion so that you will know that it is not always easy to get funds through the available sourcing fund as nobody will want to put funds in a project that they are not sure of getting back their money and making gain from it. So, before looking at the various funding sources, I will first of all provide you with the formula of determining how much you can gain from your money. Knowing this will help you to ascertain how easy or difficult it will be for you to access funds. It will also help you to speak convincingly to the funding sources you want to use.

Determining the amount your movie will make

It is simple to calculate the amount of money you will make from your movie. The mathematics is not complicated. It is as simple as multiplying the number of viewers you are expecting by the cost of per view. You should be realistic with your price per view regardless of the medium through which your film will be displayed to the viewers. This is because the movie industry is very competitive. Your movie is competing not just with the current movies but also the past and future movies, movie makers, TV series, marketers and in fact the entire participants in the marketing aspect of movie making.

The point I am trying to make here is that the cost of viewing a movie is not something that is static. But it is not completely flexible. You should be sensible about it. Whether you want to sell higher or lower, your price should reflect what is in vogue in the industry. The average cost per view is as follows:

Cinema screen or DVD = $9.99
IPTV for a month = $9 per month ($0.3 per day)
Regular forms of television = $90 per month ($3 per day)
Amazon rental = $1.99 to $2.99 per rental.

As I mentioned above, the cost per view is not static and not very flexible. This is because prices are determined by the market forces and economics regardless of the type of movie you want to make. Consequently, a sure way of increasing the income you will make from your movie is to make effort to increase the number of viewers you have. If you have a reasonable number of viewers, you will definitely make enough money from your movie. Therefore, pay more attention in increasing the number of your viewers than on the price. Your viewers are your audience. As normal in every manufacturing process, you don't get into filmmaking without knowing who your audience is. It is also not enough to know who they are. You should also know the best ways of reaching them. If you know who your audience is and you know how to reach them, it will be easier for you to determine the amount you will make from each movie. Your audience size is the amount you will make from your movie and you should make your budget in accordance with that.

Now that you know who they are and how to reach them, the problem to contend with is how to increase the number of your viewers. It is simple. The best way of getting more viewers or making people spend their money on your movie is to provide them with quality films. If they like your work, they will definitely spend their money on it. Besides, people that have watched your movie and like it will definitely refer other people to it. In a similar manner, if you have good work, it will also be easier for you to get crowdfunding. You may be wondering how crowdfunders will know the quality of your work when this is your first project. I will explain more on this in another chapter. But suffice it to mention that you need to write a quality book and concentrate on making your book popular. If you have a hot selling literary work, it is likely that many investors will like to invest in the project of making the film.

Various Film Financing Models

Below are some of the traditional means of financing the making of movies which are still used today.

Government grants

Governments of various countries have different funding programs for filmmakers and producers. If you want to produce a film, I will advise you to take time to research on various government funding programmes for filmmakers in your country. In the subsequent subheading, I will list some of these funding sources of various countries. Most governments give out loans or grants to filmmakers in order to boost tourism in their countries and also to improve their economy. The film industry is an economy driven industry. It drives the economy in different ways. Countries with strong movie industries are likely to make huge amounts of money from it and other related sectors such as tourism, real estate and hotels. Another reason why many governments provide filmmakers with grants is because they believe that it will create jobs for their citizens and also bring in talented individuals into their society. It is also a veritable means of promoting the culture of a society to the world. Shooting a film in a particular location is a great means of showcasing the place to the entire world. In the US, states such as Utah, Pennsylvania, New Mexico, Oklahoma, Connecticut, New York, Louisiana, Ohio and Georgia provide certain forms of incentives to producers that shoot their films in their states. In the UK, the British Film Institute is a governmental institution that oversees the affairs of the filmmakers. The institute also provides certain forms of funding, grants or financial assistance to film producers in the UK. The government spends a huge sum of money running into tens of millions on filmmaking in the country through the BFI. In Europe, there are also similar government programmes that help budding filmmakers to achieve their dreams

So, if there are grants available for film producers in your country, you can try to avail yourself of such opportunity. It is the best form of funding sources to avail yourself because in most cases no financial returns are required and no collateral will be expected from you. It will be issued to you if you meet the requirements. The only disadvantage of this kind of grant is that the process of getting it can be boring and daunting. This is because it involves a lot of bureaucracy which may take a long time to be completed. Some applicants who are not used with such bureaucracy can easily lose patience and look for alternative funding sources. If you are going to apply for any government grant, I will advise you to first study the programme and find out what it is all about and the best way go about it before submitting your application. Always ensure that you support your application with the right documentations to facilitate approval and reduce or eliminate the possibility of your application being rejected.

Tax incentives

Some governments also support filmmakers and all other forms of creative industries by giving them cash or tax incentives. Tax incentives are forms of government sponsorship programmes aimed at attracting filmmakers or encouraging and promoting creativity and achieving other aims mentioned above. The government of certain Canadian Provinces as well as some US states as mentioned above provide certain tax incentives of about 15% to 70% for production, labour and services on films and other forms of entertainment such as games. These forms of incentives are generally regarded as soft-money incentives. Each country or state offering this kind of incentive has her requirements for eligibility. Normally, the tax incentives are provided after the interactive or theatrical production has been accomplished. People that will receive these payments are expected to live within the states or provinces offering them. Some states will also require the filmmakers to shoot certain or all portions of their movie within their boundaries while provide such subsidies for any movies shot within the state facilities regardless of where they are located. Such facilities include studios, agents, sound stages, brokers, agencies, hotels, catering companies, rental facilities, insurance companies and banks.

Like the Canadian Provinces and some US states, the German government also offers tax incentives to filmmakers in the country through what is known as the tax shelters. According to the German law, filmmakers and investors in the industry are entitled to instant tax deduction for their films whether it has gone for production or not or whether it is a German production or not. The law also makes it possible for film producers to sell the copyright to their productions to the tax shelters for the amount the film is budgeted at and then lease back from tax shelters at the cost that is around 89 percent of the initial cost. With this incentive, a producer can make up to $10 million from a large budget movie of $100 million. The profit does not include the cost for legal and middlemen services.

The German government has other incentives meant for producers. The funding programme which is known as the German Federal Film Fund is sponsored by the German Federal Commissioner for Culture and the Media and meant to provide financial assistance to film producers. But the producers are required to satisfy certain conditions in order to be eligible for funding. For example, to qualify for the programme, a producer has to pass the cultural eligibility test. The website for the programme is www.germanfilmfinance.com which has a feature that filmmakers can use to determine their eligibility for accessing the funds.

In the UK, there is a similar funding programme. Unlike the German tax shelter where the law does not require the producer of the film to shot the film in Germany, the UK tax shelters require producers to shoot at least some portion of the movie in the UK. It also requires producers to have film crew that consists of a significant number of UK actors and players in the industry. Under the British tax shelters, producers can also sell their copyright to a British company for an additional $10 million to be raised. This is the main reason why some American filmmakers produce their movies in the UK studios such as Pinewood and Shepperton.

If you are planning to move into filmmaking or adapt your book to a film, you should consider funding the project with these kinds of tax incentives if there are any available in your country. The problem with this funding source is that, the producer may end up losing a significant portion of their profits to middlemen and agents that provide certain services to them. For example, you will need an accountant to handle the finance for you as well as a lawyer to deal with the legal aspects. In the end, you will have to settle your bill with a significant portion of your profit.

Crowdfunding

Crowdfunding is now growing in popularity. Many entrepreneurs and start-ups are funding their new businesses through crowdfunding. In crowdfunding, consumers and investors themselves provide funds for the execution of the project but they get back their money and returns when the project starts to sell. It works in a similar manner with shares. You invest in a business and then get a share from the profits generated from the business. There are today a number of movies that were funded through these means. Some of the crowdfunded films include Anomalisa, Manthan, Star Trek: Renegades, Iron Sky, Veronica Mars, Kung Fury, Code 8 and others. There are a number of online sources that now provide crowdfunding opportunities. Some of the crowdfunding websites are IndieGoGo and KickStarter.

Private equity financing

Private equity financing is a direct opposite of the government funding sources. Unlike the government funding programmes, the finance here is provided by private establishments and private individuals who in turn receive tax advantages. There are various reasons why people will invest in a movie. Some people invest in a movie because they have strong belief that they will recoup their money and make some profits from it. They can also invest in such a business as a means of obtaining a tax advantage. For example, if you are provided with financial assistance by a private equity financing establishment, the investor will get tax incentives equal to the amount provided as well as state tax and pre-sale credits. If you find individuals that are willing to provide you with funds, you should consider taking advantage of such an opportunity. However, before you access such a fund ensure that you have your plan for your distribution. Also bear in mind that private equity financiers rarely provide financial assistance to a person twice. This is a little bit of a disadvantage on your side and it will require you to start building a new relationship with another fund provider in your second project, if you have any.

Private investors

There are a lot of private investors that invest their money in other people's establishments with the intention of making gains from their investments when the business begins to yield profit. Some of these private investors are interested in the movie industries and can sponsor filmmakers to produce their films, especially if the chances of the movies selling quickly are high.

Television pre-sales

This is a method of financing a film project by selling the TV rights to an interested party and receiving the payment upfront. This means you will be paid for the TV rights before the film is produced. The money you receive from the sales will be used to sponsor or fund the project. Most of the television stations that purchase such rights are wings of the parent company of the movie studios selling the rights. However, under normal circumstances, the television rights are sold after the production of the movie but when production fund is an issue, it can be sold before the film is made.

Pre-sales

As the name suggests, you can raise money for the production of a film by selling the distribution rights to interested parties in various locations ahead of the production of the film. It works in a similar manner with TV right except that here what the investor purchases is the right to be the distributor of the film in various locations. After obtaining the distribution right, the producers will be obliged by the distributor to hand over certain elements of the content and cast to ensure that they are not modified or altered in any way. The distributor can stop providing the filmmakers with finance if the material is altered in any form. Certain decisions about the casting are often taken by the distributors and the sales manager so as to obtain the marquee names required for attracting an international audience.

The company that is buying the distribution right can, during negotiation, include a clause in the contract that will allow them to terminate the deal or to withdraw funding if any of the big name actors or directors that are supposed to be involved in the project pulls out and the producers are not able to provide a suitable replacement. Normally, the distributor will be required to make a 20% payment into the filmmaker's account after sealing the deal. The remaining percentage will be made available to the producer as soon as they complete the project and hand over the film to foreign sales agents. Normally, a producer enters this type of a contract in order to obtain a production loan from a bank using the value of the contract as collateral. Note that the distribution rights are sold territory by territory or to different distributors for different territories. For example, a business or an individual can purchase the right to be the distributor of a film in New York and another purchases the right to distribute it to consumers in New Jersey.

Negative pickup deal

This method of financing is an option for independent filmmakers or producers. In this option, an independent film producer and a movie studio agree on a deal in which the studio accepts to pay a stipulated amount to the producer for the purchase of a movie. The payment also has to be made within a specified period of time. Before the date stipulated on the contract, it is the responsibility of the producer to handle all expenses. The contract will also oblige the producer to pay for any additional expenses not captured in the budget. In other words, the filmmaker will source for finance to make the film and after making the film, they will sell the right of ownership to any studio or distributor that wants it. The buyer will become the owner of the movie.

Product placement financing

Product placement is a veritable means of getting more funds for the production of a movie. In this method, the producers of the movie will agree to advertise a product in their movies in exchange for some money. This method is a good option for producers that have some funds already but are still in need for more money. They will complete what is left to fund their filmmaking project with the money they create from the adverts. It is possible to advertise more than one product or service in a movie. Multiple product advertising can increase the income generated through this means.

Product placements can take different forms apart from advertising a product. It can occur in the form of trade by barter where you use a facility or equipment and compensate the owner by showing their products or services in the movie. For example, you can shoot in a restaurant or in a hotel and rather than paying them for the use of their facility, you will reach at an agreement with them to show their hotel in the movie. Finding a business to barter with may not be a difficult deal because many businesses see it as an opportunity to use what they have to get what they don't have or to receive a service without paying any other money. However, if you want to barter, you have to be very careful with it. Don't give false hope or oversell your film to a business that you will want to barter with. Overselling your business is tantamount to making false promises. It is even better to make little promises and deliver more than you promise. If you are a movie enthusiast, it is highly probable that you have seen a movie with advert or a movie where a facility is used and clearly shown so that the viewers will see it. This is a typical example of product placement. The producers of Minority Report obtained funds reportedly amounting to $20 million from American Express and Lexus to showcase their products.

A company can also provide a filmmaker with some items or materials they will require for the shooting of their movies for their products to be advertised in the movie. Contributions that can be made include cars, computer, hotel accommodations, costumes and other. These material contributions are not money in the real sense but they help the producers to save money. They will save the money required for the renting of the product.

Bridge financing

Bridge financing is a short-term financing method in which a filmmaker obtains a loan or equity from an investment bank or a venture capital firm. The loan is meant to help the producer of a movie to start its project until a longer-term financing option is obtained. It is therefore an interim fund, which will serve a filmmaker for the mean time until they get a permanent financing option. The term is also known as bridging loan, swing loan and caveat loan. Producers utilise this short term financing option when they are yet to obtain fund from their major sponsor but they have an urgent need for money to accomplish certain aspects of the movie. For example, it can be used by a producer in a situation where they need money to accomplish certain things required of them by their investors as conditions for financing their film project.

Gap/supergap financing

In this financing method, a producer obtains a loan from a lender using the film's unsold rights as well as territories as security for the loan. It attracts higher fees and interest rates because investors consider it as a very risky investment. However, the producer still benefits from that because they are required to pay about 220 to 30 percent equity in order to obtain the loan. It works in similar manner with a real estate mortgage loan.

Apart from these traditional financing options, there are other ways of financing a film project. For example, you can utilise your personal savings if it is big enough. But this option is not a feasible one for beginners in the industry. Only a few individuals may have personal savings that are huge enough as to fund the making of a movie. You can also borrow money from your friends and relatives if they are wealthy and willing to give. Seeking for financial assistance from friends and relatives is good if you have wealthy friends and family members. This is because you will obtain the help at a favourable term. Secondly, you will not be under tension to repay the money. Besides, the process of getting such financial assistance is not all that complicated and difficult. It is devoid of complex paperwork and documents because it is more of an informal arrangement. However, the problem with such a financing option is that it is not easy to find a friend that is willing to give such assistance, especially if the amount required is huge.

Note that each of these financing options has its own strengths and drawbacks, which you must consider if you want to make use of any of them. Another important point to bear in mind is that it is your situation, the type of movie project that you are embarking on, your locality and other factors that will determine which financing option is the most suitable means for you. In the coming subheading, I am going to a list and explain the various organisations and agencies that provide financial assistance to beginners in the movie industry in various Western countries. It will be good that you know these financial sources in case you need their help.

Funding Sources for Various Countries

As I mentioned above, virtually every country has organisations that provide funding for filmmaking. Some of the organisations are owned by the government, while some are owned by private individuals and establishments. It is good that you know these organisations if you are planning to adapt your book into a movie as they may be of help to you. Here are the important ones in some countries with well developed movie industries.

Organisations in the UK

British Film Institute, normally abbreviated as BFI, is the main government institution that provides financial assistance to filmmakers in a number of ways. It is the organisation that oversees the distribution of lottery funds for films. The institution has various kinds of programmes aimed at providing financial aid to film producers. Some of financial support programmes of BFI include BFI Vision Awards for rewarding new generation film production companies as well as producers. Visit the website of the organisation www.bfi.org.uk to learn about their activities and funding programmes. Its website has a funding finder guide that you can use to find out the various funding programmes and opportunities for new comers in the movie industries including budding writers, directors, producers and actors who require help with their short film. There are also funding programmes for newbies in the industry that will want to advance in their profession.

Creative England

Creative England is another organisation that works for the development and growth of independent creative businesses. They also help talented participants in the independent creative businesses. However, the organisation only nurtures talents within England. It has initiated various programmes through which it provides financial assistance to talents and new comers in the England's creative industry including the gaming, film, tech and TV industries. If you are in England, you should avail yourself of the funding opportunities provided by this institute. The institute also connects beginners and talented creative minds with well established organisations that can be of help to them. Find more about the institution at www.creativeengland.co.uk.

Creative Europe Desk UK

This organisation has offices in the four nations that make up the United Kingdom. The organisation provides detailed information about the Creative Europe through seminars, workshops and conferences. They also provide useful information about funding opportunities in the industries via their website www.creativeeuropeuk.eu/. Go through their website to learn about their activities and how they will be of help to you. You can also sign up for their e-newsletters for updates. Newbies in the creative industry can also contact the office of Creative Europe Desk UK for advice and guidelines. The organisations have offices in London, Edinburgh, Belfast, Cardiff, Manchester and Glasgow. Their funding opportunities are available for various talents in different aspects of the entertainment and creative industry including film and TV producers, sales agents, film distributors, video game developers, film markets, organisers of film festivals, cinema exhibitors, film education specialists and others.

Creative Scotland

Creative Scotland has the same objectives as Creative England but it is for talents in Scotland. It is a public organisation that provides help in various ways to growing artists, writers, film producers, screen artists and other talented individuals in the creative industry. The organisation helps people with ideas to actualise them and bring them to the level of reality. It obtains funds from the National Lottery and Scottish Government and makes it available to talented individuals in the creative industry who need them to bring their ideas to reality. The organisation also provides supports and financial assistance to producers of short and feature films.

Ffilm Cymrum Wales

The Ffilm Cymrum Wales is a public body in Wales that works for the development of the film industry in the country in order to bring about economic, cultural and educational growth. The agency provides financial help and funding to beginners and stakeholders in the Wales movie industry. There are financial programmes for writers, producers, directors and other talented individuals in the film industry for the development and production of movies. Besides financial assistance, the industry also provides mentoring services to growing talents. The organisation also helps filmmakers and distributors to sell their products to their target audience. They do this by encouraging the use of films and visual components for teaching and for other education purposes as well as community regeneration. They also promote films among consumers encouraging them to visit cinema and other movie venues.

Film London

Film London is the screen industries agency in London that provides support to creative minds in the city to enable them to bring their ideas to reality. They have various kinds of funding programmes for budding talents in gaming, television, animation and film industries. The agency also provides training and mentoring opportunities to beginners in the filmmaking industry of London. It also encourages investors to invest their money in the creative industry of the capital city of England. The various support programmes offered by this agency include Prestigious London Calling, training, financing and distribution schemes and events, the Feature Funding Scheme Microwave, Production Finance Market, Familiarisation Trips for Overseas executives, and London Calling Plus Short Film Schemes.

Northern Ireland Screen

It is a public agency in Northern Ireland that works for the growth of the film, digital content and television industries as channels for improving the region's economy and promoting the culture of the people to the entire world. The organisation also aims at improving the education of children with visual technology and contents. Backed by the government of the region, the agency offers supports to the growing talents in the country's screen industry through a number of her funding programmes and schemes for the various aspects of the industry including the following:
- custom-built studio facilities
- production and development funding for film, television and digital content
- marketing of Northern Ireland as a global location for film production and promotion of her talents and products
- information and locations services and production support for filming in the country
- training and skill acquisition and development financial assistance encouraging investment in film education, archive, heritage and skill development
- production funding for Irish Language and many more.

Other resources that filmmakers and those in the creative industries in the country can take advantage of include, but are not limited to, the following:

- BBC Films
- Channel 4
- Cinema and Television Benevolent Fund
- iFeatures
- Kickstarter
- Indiegogo
- SDI (Scottish Documentary Institute)
- Wellcome Trust and others

Note that some of these institutions and organisations may not provide financial support but they support the filmmaking industries and the participants in it in other ways such as providing free advice and mentoring services, guidance, connection with the stakeholders in the industry, promotion of products and others. Even if you don't have any need for financial assistance, there are other ways through which you can benefit from them.

Resources and Funding Sources for Filmmakers in Australia

Australia's government has shown great support to filmmaking in the country right from the early beginning of the cinema industry in the country. She has provided support in different forms to her film and entertainment industry in order to drive economy, boost tourism, provide employment and also bring in more talent into the industry. Here are some of the film funding sources in Australia.

Screen Australia

This is an organisation that provides useful resources and financial incentives to filmmakers and distributors that specialise in Australian screen content. The objective of this institution is to promote and popularise the Australian stories and culture among screen audiences and film enthusiasts across the globe. The institution has instituted a number of funding programmes and other useful resources to enable filmmakers and talents with ideas on the Australian society to actualise their dreams. Some of the popular programmes of the agency include Co-production Programmes and Producer Offset. Application for financial assistance can be made via the organisation's website www.screenaustralia.gov.au. Note that this institution was established in 2008 with a merger of Film Finance Corporation, the Australian Film Commission and Film Australia. It is a public agency funded by the Australian government. It is also sponsoring TV series such as TV dramas.

Screenwest

Screenwest is an organisation aimed at providing financial support for the producers of feature films and television in Australia. It also promotes Australian films and ensures that they get to the right audience. The agency which belongs to the Western Australian government partners with the screen industry to work for the development and growth of the film, digital media and television production in that part of Australia. The agency also extends its support and funding outside Western Australia to any indigenous and factual production. You can obtain more information about the agency from their website www.screenwest.wa.gov.au.

Screen Territory

This is a useful resource for screen industries in the Northern Territory of Australia. It is a government owned agency that promotes the development of the cinema industry as well as other creative industries in that region of Australia. Its website https://screenterritory.nt.gov.au/about contains useful information about its activities and operations. In summary, it has a number of grant programmes through which it offers financial support to individuals going into the movie industries including scriptwriters. This agency discharges its function with the aim of popularising the cultural identity of the region and also to provide employment to people going into the area. It also supports the creative and screen industry so as to improve the export potentials of the industry and also to encourage investors to pull their resources in the sector.

Screen Queensland

This is another government owned agency that offers some financial assistance and useful resources to the screen industry in Queensland in order to bring about the growth and development of the industry through film and television projects. The agency has a website which contains useful information about the mission and vision statements of the agency as well as current funding programmes available for filmmakers and talented individuals in the industry to access. Take a look at http://screenqueensland.com.au/ to find out more about how Screen Queensland will be of help to you if you are living within the territory.

ScreenAct

ScreenAct is another resource for talented individuals in the Australian cinema industry to make use of. Its objective is to grow and develop the industry in the country by providing funding or financial aid to talents in the industry including screenplay writers and authors planning to adapt their books into movies. The agency executes projects such as script development that will bring about the development of screen industry in the country. ScreenAct is located in Canberra the capital city of Australia.

ScreenWest

The Western Australian public agency that provides funding, resources and other kinds of support to the individuals going into the screen industry is known as the ScreenWest. The agency strives to promote and develop the creative industry by providing necessary aids and financial support for the execution of digital media, film and television projects. It does not only sponsor screen production but also drama, factual and indigenous production. It has introduced different funding and support programs for newbies and old time players in the industry. Find out more about these programmes from www.screenwest.com.au which is the official website of the agency.

Screen Tasmania

Screen Tasmania belongs to the government of Tasmania. Through the agency, the government of the state provides support to television and multimedia industries in the states. It achieves this objective by increasing the amount of independent screen production that takes place in the country. The agency takes the lead in ensuring that the industry grows. It is also its responsibility to spot opportunities in the industry and also to develop the key areas of the screen industry. In the area of finance, filmmakers can access grants, loans and equity investment offered by the agency for the development, production and marketing of screen projects such as documentaries, drama, short films, digital media, TV series and feature films in the state.

South Australian Film Corporation (SAFC)

South Australian government supports filmmaking in the state and provides funds for the production of outstanding films and television programmes that showcase the Australian culture and creative mind and that will also bring some economic benefits to the country. The government makes the funds available through a number of programmes and financial aid opportunities made available by the South Australian Film Corporation. Visit the institution's website http://www.safilm.com.au/#funding to learn more about the state film funding programmes.

There are other resources and funding sources available in Australia apart from those mentioned above. A lot of nongovernmental organisations as well as state government agencies provide aid to talented individuals wanting to build a career for themselves in the industry. A good number of universities and higher education institutions in the country give scholarships and grants for screenplay writing. Typical examples of such organisations include the Australian Writers' Guild, Screen & Media Industry Development Organisation, Writers' Centres and Residences and others. Use the Internet to find out more about available funding programmes for participants in the industry in order to see which one will suit your project or that you qualify for. Be sure that you subscribe for the newsletter of a number of them so that you will be among the first to know when there is a new funding programmes.

Competition in the screen industry of Australia

Some institutions also offer screenplay writing competitions to talented writers and reward them with cash prizes and incentives. Such contest and competition is a veritable means through which the society helps talented individuals to develop their creative minds and skills. If you are good in writing scripts for films, you can also participate in the programme as a means of making money with your talents. Joining in the programme is also a veritable means of improving on your skills. You can find out about such competition from the industry journals such as Inside Film (IF), Encore, newsletters of the various organisations and agencies that provide such opportunities.

US Funding Sources and Resources

United States of America is another country that has a lot of government programmes aimed at developing the cinema industry and helping creative minds with ideas to bring them to reality. Almost all the states in the country have government agencies that support the film, screen, TV and gaming industries in various ways including provision of financial assistance and other useful resources such as mentorship, guidance, facility, connection, useful information and others. Regardless of the state you are residing in, there are resources and funding opportunities to avail yourself of insofar as you have the talents needed in the industry. Here, we are going to examine a few of them, especially government sponsored organizations and agencies as it is outside of the scope of this book to explain them all. To find more of them on the Internet, just choose any search engine of your choice and type "Film fund in the United States of America". You will definitely get some positive and impressive results from the search.

Virginia Film Office

Virginia is one of the states in the United States of America that support the movie industry in a number of ways. The government of the country has an agency known as Virginia Film Office, which has the responsibility of growing and developing the state's film and art industry. The office helps the creative industry with funds in order to make film production in the state very much affordable. Filmmakers in the state enjoy tax exemption. The state also provides sales support. The activities of the office, which was established in 1980, help to generate revenue to the state as well.

Film SF

Film SF is a San Francisco institution that provides support for all types of productions in the creative industry including feature films, music videos, student films, documentaries, feature films, commercial films and student films. Filmmakers and growing talents in the industry can access a lot of incentives from them. The institution has a website filmsf.org which provides useful information about the film making industry of the state. For example, you will be able to find good locations for film shooting in the state from their website. You can also find out the available incentives for filmmakers from their website. So, take time to go through the website to find out how the institution will be of help to you if you are living in the state.

Oregon Film

Oregon Film has the responsibility of growing and developing the cinema industry as well as the film, interactive, animation, video and creative content industries in the state. It achieves this aim in a number of ways, which include providing incentives to filmmakers and talented individuals in the industries. Their funding programmes include film, TV and media incentives of about 20% rebate of all productions based on Oregon. The institution will also offer a cash payment of about 16.2% of the total cost of wages to participants and actors in the state. The state also does not charge any sales tax on movie products in the state. The state also provides a variety of shooting locations to experienced crew.

Pennsylvania Film Office

Just like other state agencies that provide support to the creative industry, the Pennsylvania Film Office has the aim of building a strong local movie industry, which generates revenue to the state and creates more jobs into job seekers in the state. The organisation also has the objective of fostering innovation in the cinema industry of the state. The institution also assists filmmakers by helping them to find locations suitable for the shooting of their films. They work with experts that provide production guidance, helping them to establish strong crew that consists of talented individuals.

Rhode Island Film & TV Office

Rhode Island is one of the smallest states in the United States of America. The government of the state establishes the Film $ Television Office in order to enhance the reputation of the state as a nice location for film and television projects. Besides, the agency provides support to the artists and filmmakers in the state in various ways, especially by providing them with financial support. They also provide production. You can check their website www.film.ri.gov/ to know more about their operations and the various ways you can benefit from them.

Other government agencies that offer incentives and various kinds of support to filmmakers in the USA are as follows:
- Oklahoma Film and Music Office
- North Carolina Film Office
- New Mexico State Film Office
- NY Governor's Office for Motion Picture and Television Development
- South Carolina Film Office
- Ohio Film Office
- Tennessee Film, Entertainment, and Music Commission
- Washington Filmworks
- Wyoming Film Office
- West Virginia Film Office
- Utah Film Commission
- Virgin Islands Film Office
- Texas Film Commission
- New Jersey Motion Picture and Television Commission
- St. Petersburg/Clearwater, Florida Film Commission
- Florida Office of Film & Entertainment
- New Hampshire Film & Television Office
- Montana Film Office
- Mississippi Film Office
- Louisiana Entertainment
- Kentucky Film Office
- California Film Commission
- Colorado Office of Film, Television & Media
- Arkansas Production Alliance and many more

Apart from these public owned agencies, there are other private organisations and foundations in the US that offer incentives and various kinds of support to film makers. You can also see if you will be lucky to get their funding and assistance. Some of the foundations include:

- Jerome Foundation
- Heinz Endowment
- United States Artists
- Women in Film
- Surdna Foundation
- Time Warner Foundation
- Tribeca Film Institute and others

Film Funding Programmes for Canadian Movie Industries

Whether you are planning to make a feature, short or documentary film, there are a number of funding programmes and resources made available both by the Canadian government and private organisations and foundations. Use any of the search engines you are comfortable with to look for such funding and initiatives in research, you are definitely going to find one that will suit the type of project that you want to embark on. Here are some of the popular ones that you should know.

Note that there are funding opportunities in all Canadian provinces, even though Ontario and British Columbia are the two major centres of the Canadian movie and entertainment industry. Some of the agencies also provide filmmakers with post production and marketing financial assistance and advice. In other words, there are multiple ways of getting help and resources in the Canadian movie industry. Below are some of the notable government programmes and initiatives for filmmakers in the industry.

Telefilm

Telefilm is one of the Canadian institutions that provide support to film industries. It is a funding agency of the Canadian government. It is under the management of the Ministry of Canadian Heritage. It has its headquarters in Montreal with branches in other locations such as Vancouver, Ontario, Quebec, Halifax, Nova Scotia, British Columbia, Toronto and others. The organisation was established in 1967. The institution has the objective of helping emerging artists to achieve their potential. It has financial assistance programmes for television, media and feature films. Besides these schemes, the institution has other support programmes for filmmakers such as development and promotion programmes.

Canada Council for the Arts

The Canada Council for the Arts is the national funder for film and art industries in the country. The institution is responsible for growing and raising the status of the Canadian art by providing financial assistance such as grants and other forms of incentives and services through a number of their programmes. They make payment available for the artists and art organisations in Canada. The institution also funds research in the field as well as other aspects of art and entertainment like dance, theatre and television programmes. You can apply for a grant or funding directly from the organisation's website at http://canadacouncil.ca/funding/grants. Take a look at the website to know what it is all about and how they will be of help to you. But be aware that the Canada Council for Arts plays emphasis on expertise and innovation.

BravoFact

BravoFact, like the other organisations, exists to help creative and talented individuals in the short film and video industries. It was established in 1995 to fund the production of short movies regardless of their subject matters, styles and genres. The organisation also offers support to personnel in drama, animation, comedy, dance and other forms of entertainment. The foundation has provided financial assistance for the execution of more than 1,500 short films through the company. It is now regarded as the largest funder of short films in the entire country. BravoFact is a division of Bell Media owned by BCE Inc.

The Canadian Television Fund (CTF)

The Canadian Television Fund, which runs an annual budget of about $265 million, is a public/private partnership in Canada that assists filmmakers and other personnel in the movie and entertainment industries financially to enable them to execute their projects. The institution receives support from the Canadian government and cable companies and direct-to-home satellite service providers. Since the establishment of this organisation, it has financed a lot of movie production as well as TV programmes of various genres such as drama, documentaries, children's show and others. English, French and Aboriginal languages are used in some of the programmes sponsored by the organisation.

Hot Docs

Hot Docs is another funder of the Canadian movies. It also provides support to international documentary projects. Since it was established, it has given out about $3.9 million in loans and grants without charging any interest on them. The organisation has sponsored 187 projects in the industry. It also provides other forms of assistance and services like pitching and training services. You can apply for any of the support you want directly from the website of the association. Visit https://www.hotdocs.ca/i/film-funds to find out more about the organisation and how they will be of help to you.

The OMDC Film Fund

This funding programme is reserved for filmmakers in Ontario. The institution is a funder of feature film projects in their final development and production financing stages. The fund has two aspects, the development and production. Each of these two aspects work in a unique manner. In the development aspect, the institution provides a loan of up to $25,000 for the completion of the final development stage. The loan does not attract any interest. The product aspect of the programme provides filmmakers with $400,000 repayable advance to be used for the completion of a feature film.

Apart from the public owned institutions that support filmmaking industries with finance and useful resources, there are other organisations and institutions that also help to boost film production in the country. Some of these institutions and funders are as follows:
- Independent production fund
- Cogeco program development fund
- Le Fonds Harold Greenberg
- Nova Scotia Independent Production Fund
- Remstar's Fund
- Quebecor Fund
- Rogers Documentary Fund
- Saskatchewan Film and Video Development Corporation
- Shaw Rocket Fund
- Small Market Local Programming Fund
- The Telus Fund

International Grant and Funding Programs for Filmmakers

On the international level, here are some film grant funding programmes that you should avail yourself of if you are innovative and have good screenplay or book to turn into a movie abound.

Warner Brothers Television Directors and Writers Workshops

The Warner Brothers Television Directors and the Writers Workshops are funders for television film directors and writers respectively. The institutions offer workshops for directors and writers that were selected for financial assistance. Applicants are required to satisfy certain conditions before they are accepted. Check their website to see if you are eligible for financial help by these institutions.

Film Independent's Fast Track Fellowship

The fellowship programme is established to provide resources and financial support to budding narrative and documentary films writers, producers and directors to enable them develop their potential and bring their ideas to the level of reality. The fellowship which normally lasts for three days takes place in Los Angeles, US. Filmmakers that are accepted into the programme are entitled to $10,000 Millennium Entertainment Fellowship and $15,000 production grant provided by Alfred P. Sloan Foundation. The applicants are also required to meet certain criteria in order to be eligible for the support.

World Cinema Fund

World Cinema Fund has the objective of developing cinema culture in regions and localities with low infrastructure for filmmaking. The organisation also helps to nurture, promote and grow cultural diversity in German Cinemas. The organisation provides assistance to filmmakers that have exceptional film project with unique aesthetic and authentic cultural approach. It provides help for the production of movies that do not require extra funding in order to be produced.

The Hubert Bals Fund

It is designed to provide financial help and other forms of support to talented feature film makers from Africa, Middle East, Eastern Europe, Middle East, Latin America and Asia. Its funding programmes extend to post production activities. Successful applicants can receive up to 10,000 Euros for the development of their scripts and development project.

Other international funding institutions include the following:
- Women in Film/Netflix Finishing Fund
- The David Ross Fetzer Foundation for Emerging Artists
- US in Progress, Paris Edition
- IFP Independent Narrative Lab
- The Roy Dean Grant/From the Heart Productions
- The Jerome Foundation's Film and Video Grant Programme
- Nextpix/Firstpix Crowdfunding Grant
- Panavision's New Filmmaker Programme
- Screen Australia's Feature Funding Programme
- Metro Screen
- Jump Start Support Programme and many others.

With these international funding institutions and organisations, you stand a better chance of getting financial assistance and other forms of support for the development of and production of your script regardless of where you come from.

Companies Involved in Film Production Industry

As I have mentioned, one company does not actually make a film even if it is an independent filmmaker. Any film you see is the handiwork of a number of people. If you are entering into the movie industry, you should know these companies. You may be requiring their services if you are going to turn your book into a movie. Here are some of the popular ones.

US Film Production Companies

- Sony Pictures Entertainment

Sony Pictures Entertainment, which is normally abbreviated as SPE, is one of the well known film producing companies in the US. The company is a wing of Sony Film Holding Inc. owned by Sony Corporation of America managed by Sony Americas Holding Inc., which is a wing of Sony Corporation, a multinational technology and media conglomerate that is headquartered in Tokyo, Japan. Sony Pictures Entertainment offers a lot of services in the industry. Its services include but not limited to motion picture and television production as well as their acquisitions and distribution. They also offer digital content creation and distribution, television networks, operation of studio facilities and creation of new products, services and technologies of entertainment. The company which has its base in Culver City, California was established on 7 August 1991 and since that time, it has franchised a lot of films including *The Karate Kid*, *The Sniper*, *The Smurfs*, *Robert Langdon*, *Resident Evil* and many more. It has grown to become one of the well know film production companies. Today, it has an operation budget of $341 million; and as of 2016, it employs about 3,500 people. Visit the company's website sonypictures.com to know more about the company.

- Columbia Pictures Industries, Inc.

Columbia Pictures, also called Columbia or Columbia Pictures for short, is a part of Sony Pictures Motion Picture Group which is a subsidiary of Sony Pictures of Sony Entertainment owned by Sony. Harry Cohn and Jack Cohn (Harry's brother) and Joe Brandt established the company on 19 June 1981 and named it CBC Film Sales Corporation. But six years later, it was renamed Columbia Pictures. In 1924, it became a public traded company. Today, Columbia Pictures operates a film studio. It produces and distributes films. The company has grown into one of the world's largest film studios. It is a part of the famed "Big Six" major American film studios.

- Affir Films

Affir Films specialises in the production of evangelical Christian drama Biblical films and Kid and Family movies. Affir Films is a subsidiary of Sony Pictures Entertainment with Sony Pictures Worldwide Acquisitions as the parent company. The company has labelled a number of titles including *Soul Surfer*, *Faith Like Potatoes*, *Facing the Giants*, *When The Game Stand Tall*, *Fireproof* and a number of biblical characters.

- TDJ Enterprises

TDJ Enterprises is a business that belongs to Bishop TD Jakes, the owner of Potter's House. Jakes is well known in the US for its eloquence, plays, books, movies, festivals and conference. TGDJ Enterprises is into film and music production. It has existed for up to two decades and within its years of existence, the company has published a lot of films and music. Some of the prominent movie stars that feature in the company's production include Morris Chestnut, Kevin Hart, Julie Bowen, Greg Kinnear, Angela Bassett and Whitney Houston.

- Franklin Entertainment

Franklin Entertainment is a film producing business that was established in July, 2014 by one of the accomplished Hollywood author and producer, DeVon Franklin. The company specialises in the production of Christian films and dramas. It has produced some of the well hot-selling movies such as *Miracles from Heaven*, *the Star*, *The Impossible* and others.

- Advent Film Group

Founded in 2007 by George D. Escobar and Michael Snyder as an independent business, Advent Film Group specialises in the production and distribution of Christian movies. Advent as it is shortly called has published a number of Christian related movies since it was established. Some of its films include *Alone Yet Not Alone*, *Come What May* and *The Hero* which was produced in September 2014. Besides video production, Advent Film Group also supports growing talented Christian actors to be filmmakers through their training programmes. The company is based in Purcellville, Virginia, United States of America. You can find more information about their operations and services from their website http://www.adventfilmgroup.com/AFGSite/Home.html.

The above mentioned movie production companies are just few of the US based companies that are into the production and distribution of various kinds of movies. There are plenty of them. A search on any of your favourite search engine will give impressive results on this. Wikipedia has an article that contains a comprehensive list of filmmaking companies in the United States of America. Click on this link to read the article https://en.wikipedia.org/w/index.php?title=Category:Film_production_companies_of_the_United_States&pageuntil=Culver+Studios#mw-pages.

Film Production Companies in the UK

The United Kingdom is another country with a large and advanced movie industry. The British cinema industry has plenty of film producing businesses as well film distributors, script writing companies, cinematographers, studios and various establishments that handle various aspects of movie production. If you have a good book to adapt into a movie or screenplay to sell, you are sure to find a company that will accept to produce the film for you. Here are some of the UK companies that are into movie productions.

- Aardman Animations

Aardman Animations, Ltd., called Aardman for short is a British company established in 1972 by Peter Lord and David Sproxton. The company is headquartered in Bristol where it operates an animation studio. Aardman Studios as it is also called has a number of subsidiaries which include Aardman Digital, Aardman Nathan Love, Aardman Effects, Aardman Rights, Aardman Features, Aardman Commercials, Aardman International, Aardman Commercials and Aardman Broadcast. The company has become popular for its animated films such as Flushed Away, Chicken Run and others. It's productions across the globe have generated $973.2 million. Apart from feature films, the company is also into the production of TV series/series such as *The Great Egg Race*; short films like *Wat's Pig*; Musical videos like *Gridlock* and *Sledgehammer*; and commercial films like *Hamlet*, *Lurpak*, *Domestos* and *Enterprise 64*. Browse through www.aardman.com to know more about this company and all the services it has to offer.

- Banter Media

Founded in 2009 by Liam Andrew Wright and headquartered in Manchester, Banter Media offer a number of services, which include Music recording, graphic design, digital distribution, photography, film production, new media and television programming. It has produced different kinds of movies including feature films (*Ex Cathedra*), documentary (*Green & Gold*), new media (*Streets Above*), short films (*Hulme Life*, *As We Know It* and *Daisy, Daisy*) and music videos (*Never Comes Easy by Girls That Scream* and others). The company in 2010 emerged as the Grand Jury Winner. Find out more about this company from its website http://www.bantermedia.com.

- Cake Entertainment

Cake Entertainment is a private entertainment company headquartered on the 5th Floor of 76 Charlotte Street, Fitzrovia, London W1T 4QS, England, United Kingdom. Established in 2002, Cake Entertainment is into production and distribution of films. It has a subsidiary known as TeamTO. Since it began operation in 2002, it has distributed a lot of movies such as *Total Drama*, *Stoked*, *Skunk Fu*, *The Hitchhiker's Guide to the Galaxy*, *Aifric*, *Pocoyo* and many others. It is the producer of *Poppy Cat*, *My Knight and Me*, *Bottersnikes and Gumbles* and *Angelo Rules*. Visit www.cakeentertainment.com to know more about this company and its operations.

- Idiotlamp Productions Limited

Idiotlamp Productions, Ltd., which is simply referred to as Idiotlamp, was established in 2001 as an independent production. Though, Idiotlamp is a small film production company, it has established itself in the industry with the production of short films, commercials, TV and radio programmes. Some of its commercials have been applauded and given awards by a number of institutions. Some of the company's productions include *Missing Moscow*, *My Friend* (a short documentary series aired on *Channel*), and *Where Have I Been All Your Life*. Take a look at the production website of the company http://www.idiotlamp.com/ to know more about it.

- Sands Films

Sand Films started operation in 1975 when it was established by Christine Edzard. Headquartered in Rotherhithe, London, Sands Films specialises in the production of costumes for period dramas. Though the company is a private small film production company, it operates its own workshops, soundproof stage, set construction workshop, costume department, cutting room and cinema. The company facility is a comprehensive one, as it is self-sufficient. A number of other Cinema and television companies such as C4, BBC, Talkback and others have rented its facility for their production. Find out more about the company from its website http://www.sandsfilms.co.uk/.

As mentioned above, the UK has plenty of film production companies. You can find out more of these companies from the Internet. Click on this https://en.wikipedia.org/wiki/Category:Film_production_companies_of_the_United_Kingdom to have a more comprehensive list of various companies in film production in the UK.

Canadian Film Production Companies

Canada is another country with a well developed cinema industry, as I have already explained above. There are a lot of companies that contribute to the growth of her cinema industry. No matter the industry-related services you are looking for in Canada, you will always find a company that will deliver the best services to you. Here are a few of the movie producing companies in the countries.

- Allude Entertainment

Allude Entertainment is established in 2012 by Diana Donaldson, Naim Sutherland and Marshall Axani. The company is headquartered in Vancouver where it engages in the production of narrative-driven films in collaboration with the Canadian Film Industry. The three key figures and founders of the company are professionals in filmmaking. Diana Donaldson is a producer while Marshall Axani specialises in writing movie screenplay and also in directing movie production. Prof. Naim Sutherland is a Director of Photography. Each of these individuals has received different kinds of awards for their individual projects. The three pull resources together in creating short films, feature films and other kinds of movies. Some of their short film productions are *A Clinical Diagnosis of Social Anxiety*, *A Clinical Diagnosis of: Glossophobia*, *A Clinical Diagnosis of: Acrophobia*, *Ghosts of Europe and The Vessel*. They are also the producer of a feature film titled *The Hanging Tree*. The business operates a website http://alludeentertainment.com/ where you can obtain information about their company and their services.

- Back Alley Film Productions

If you are writing script for television production, Back Alley Film Productions is one of the Canadian television production companies that you rely on. The company came into existence in 1989. Today, it has offices in some of the most popular cities in Canada including Toronto, Ontario, Quebec and Montreal. Back Alley Film Productions have successfully completed TV productions, some of which have won them some awards and some were nominated for certain industry prizes. For example, the company has received the award for the Best Performance by an Actress in a Featured Supporting Role in Dramatic Program or Series and the Best Performance by an Actress in a Leading Role in a Dramatic Program or Mini-Series. Besides TV series, its production includes non-fiction films such as *Talk 19* and *Talk 16*. Find out more about the company from its website at http://www.backalleyfilms.ca/.

- Content Television

Content Television is an independent studio that specialises in television and film production as well as film distribution. The company started operation in 1996 when it was founded by Jay Forestone. At the budding stage, it was called Fireworks Entertainment, which has become defunct due to change of ownership that occurred throughout the history of the company. Today, the headquarters of the company are in the United Kingdom, having moved from its original base in Canada. It is now a subsidiary of Content Media Corporation, a UK based company. Since its inception, it has produced and distributed a lot of films including TV shows. Some of their movies are *Rat Race, Simon Magus, Interstate 60*, Hardball, Greenfingers and others. Its TV shows are Young Dracula, Zoe Busiek: *Wild Card, Relic Hunter* to mention but a few.

- Guru Studio

Guru Studio is a privately owned animation studio in Canada. It was founded by Frank Falcone, Anne Deslauries and Chuck Gammage in 2000. Guru Studio is headquartered in Toronto, Ontario, Canada. The company has distinguished itself in the movie industry, which finds expression in the various industry awards it has received. Guru studio has also participated in a number of international film festivals. It has produced a number of films some of which are *Justin Time, Mudpit, The Bacjyardigans, PAW Patrol, The Breadwinner, True and the Rainbow Kingdom, Shimmer* and *Shine Season 1* and many more. For more information about the company's service, visit gurustudio.com.

- Impact Pictures

Impact Pictures is a privately owned film production company in Canada. Jeremy Bolt and Paul W.S. Anderson are the two founders of the company. Since it was established, it has excelled in the filmmaking industry throughout their productions. They have worked in partnership with a number of big studios in Canada such as Davis Films, Sony Pictures and Constantin Film. They have made a lot of films. Some of the films are *The Dark, Resident Evil, The Hole, Massacre Up North, There's Only One Jimmy Grimble, Stiff Upper Lips, Last Christmas, Resident Evil: Afterlife, Pandorum* and many more. Note that Impact Productions have various bases. It has bases in the United States as well as in the United Kingdom. It has websites for these bases. For more information about their services, click on http://www.imdb.com/company/co0152380/?ref_=fn_al_co_3.

The above mentioned companies are just few Canadian movie making companies. There are other ones which you will be able to find through an online search. A lot of articles have been written on that like https://en.wikipedia.org/wiki/Category:Film_production_companies_of_Canada.

Each of the Provinces in Canada are making effort to develop their cinema industry. There are film producing companies in each of them. So, no matter where you are residing in the country or the province where you prefer to shoot your movie, you will find a reliable movie production company to handle the project for you.

Australian film production companies

You can decipher from our discussion on the cinema industry that Australia has a well developed movie industry. Some of the globally acclaimed actors and studios are from that part of the world. If you are in Australia and you have a book that you would like to adapt into a movie, there are a lot of film production and distribution companies that will render you top-notch services. Below are a few of the Australian film production and distribution companies.

- Blackfella Films

Founded by Rachel Perkins in 1992, Blackfella Films is headquartered in Paddington, New South Wales, Sydney, Australia. But it has another branch in Melbourne. It specialises in the production of documentary and narrative films. It makes short and lengthy feature films and contents aired on television. Its productions dwell mainly on Australian cultures. Since its inception, it has produced a lot of films and visual contents like documentary series like *The Tall Man* and First *Australians*. They are also the producers of such TV films as *Mabo* and TV series like *Redfern Now*. You can get more information about the company and their services from their official website www.blackfellafilms.com.au.

- Films and Casting Temple Pty Ltd

Films and Casting Temple Pty Ltd is owned by Anupam Sharma who established it in 2000. The company has its base in Sydney. It specialises in film casting and also offers consultancy services. It operates from Fox Studio Australia. It dwells more on Indian cinema and Bollywood genres. Films and Casting Temple Pty Ltd has become popular in the Australian movie industry for its role in establishing a link between the cinema industry in Australia and that of India. As an international film consultancy and casting firm and pioneer of the relationship between Australia and India, it has strong connection with Global Indian Talent. It also has link with Bollywood websites in Australia.

- Kennedy Miller Mitchell

Kennedy Miller Mitchel began operation in 1978 and was initially known as Kennedy Miller. It was founded by Byron Kennedy and George Miller, after whom it was named. The business' name was elongated in 2009 with the addition of Mitchell. The company, which is headquartered in Potts Point, Sydney, Australia specialises in film, television and video game production. Its products are among the most popular in Australia. Some of its popular productions are the two *Happy Feet*, the two *Babe*, the four *Mad Max* and others. The company is regarded by many people as the most accomplished Australian film producing company. As one of the Australian oldest film producing companies, a lot of films have been credited to them.

- Sunrise Films

Sunrise Films is owned by an accomplished script writer, film producer and actor, Robert Rabiah who has won several awards and has been nominated for a number of others. The company was established in 2005 to focus on the production of films about social change. It is also into television production. A number of films such as *Down Under* (a TV series), *Antonio, Death Letter, Nothing to Declare, the Ideal Cafe* and *The Further Run* were produced by these company.

- Sunstar Entertainment

Sunstar Entertainment is a privately owned business that concentrates in the production of movies and television shows that are purely Australian in all aspects. Their productions tell more of Australian stories. Sunstar Entertainment, which was established in 2011 by Andrew Fraser and Shahen Mekertichian ,showcases talented and sporting celebrities and identities through its talent management shows.

There are other film production facilities and establishments in Australia and some of them are publicly owned. You can search for more Australian movie producing companies in any of your preferred search engines. You will get an impressive result. Wikipedia has an article that listed most of these companies check out the article on this link https://en.wikipedia.org/wiki/Category:Film_production_companies_of_A ustralia. You can also make an inquiry from some of the government sponsored agencies that we have discussed above. They may have useful information about film and television production companies.

The discussion on movie production companies brings the chapter and section to an end. The subsequent topics will be on the second section of this book, which is a very important section that can be considered the focal point of the entire book.

SECTION TWO: FROM A BOOK TO A MOVIE

There is no doubt that the reason why you purchased this book or why you are reading it is that you want to learn how to turn a hot-selling book into a movie. This is the section that will provide you with a step-by-step guide on how to go about it and achieve this dream. This implies that the preceding section and chapters within it are hot air. They are basic and provide you with important detailed information about the industry, sources of funding and resources and the various companies that provide services such as film production, animation, video and video game production service. What you have learnt above will help you to know where to look for resources and who to go to for the services you will require in order to get your book turned into a movie.

Chapter 4: The Process of Turning Your Book into a Movie

As implicit from the title of this chapter, turning a book into a movie is not an "anything goes" type of activity. There is a process that you have to follow if you want to be successful in your project. If you don't follow the process you will not realise your objective of turning your book into a movie. In this chapter, I am going to tell you how you will go about it.

Making Your Book Work First

There is the tendency to think that your book will make an excellent movie simply because it is selling very quickly. You are amazed with the number of copies that you have sold so far. The truth is that a book can sell like a hot cake and yet it will not make a good movie. This is because books and films have different markets and they are not of the same discipline. Books have "interior voice" which you have to make actionable on the screen. This is where script comes into play. I will talk more about script writing in a subsequent subheading. Suffice it to mention that you have to put your book into an actionable script before you can think of making a movie from it.

Consequently, the first question you should ask yourself when the idea of turning a book into a movie comes in your mind is: Is the book going to be a good movie? The answer is no unless it is turned into a script. So, you will need a script writer or you need to learn how to write a script if you want to save money and do it by yourself.

However, before hiring a scriptwriter or continuing with the process of turning your book into a movie, you should pay more attention to making the consumers know more about it. Your book must work first before you can make a movie from it. If you have not sold plenty of copies, make effort to sell as many copies as possible.

What is your review like? This is a very important question to ask yourself at this early stage before you can move forward with the project. It is essential that you have great reviews. If your book is selling well and you have great reviews, you will easily get an offer from producers. In other words, you will be saving yourself a lot of headaches, time, money and energy in the future if you have a wonderful book. Besides, if the source material is good and many are purchasing it, a good number of the consumers who are movie enthusiasts will want to purchase the movie when it eventually sees the light of the day.

Turning Your Book into a Screenplay

Do I actually need to create a screenplay from my book? Why can't I send my book to a movie producer as it is so that they will develop the script by themselves and produce a movie with it? These are some of the questions many authors that want to adapt their books into movies ask. I have partly answered these questions in the preceding discussion on "making your book work" first. Movies and books have different languages. Books are not in actionable language and therefore, you have to create your script to make the book actionable. Another reason why you are supposed to develop your book into a script or screenplay is because movie makers don't read books. However, some publishers and studios have teams of experts that search for great selling books for them. When they find such books, they will present them to filmmakers and directors to look into them. You can see why it is important that you make your book work first. If you have a successful book, it is likely that such studios will be happy to turn it into a movie.

Screenplay, also known as a script, is what is acted and not the book itself which does not have the language of films. If you succeed in making your book work, the next task before you is to write the screenplay. The screenplay is a very important aspect of filmmaking because it is the script that is acted. So, if you get it right, the job is half done. Given its importance, it is not something that you can do anyhow. It requires expertise. There are talented and well trained scriptwriters today. You can hire the services of one of them or write it yourself. Tips for each of the options are given below.

Writing it yourself

As I mentioned above, you can turn your book into a script by yourself if you have the required skills and knowledge. Note if you don't have a good screenplay, you may not realise your dream of turning your book into a movie no matter how well it is selling. This is because many studios and film producing businesses judge the quality of your work based on the quality of your screenplay as it is what they are working on. So, if you prefer writing it yourself, it is of crucial importance that you do it very well.

I will advise you not to write your script by yourself if you have no training for that or if you have not attended film school. That you are a good book writer does not mean that you can write a screenplay very well. Screenplay has its format and language as well as method of writing it. If you follow the methodology but do not use the required actionable language, your script is lacking as well. Similarly, if you use the right language but fail to format it properly, it is also considered insufficient script. Thus, to have a quality screenplay implies that you have to get all aspects right. In summary, don't write your script by yourself unless you:

- did a study programme on that or you are a student or graduate of film college with all the necessary qualifications and skills.
- are a skilful screenplay writer or you have been into scriptwriting as a career
- are willing to learn how to do it and you have the time to learn it
- have screenplay software for formatting
- know the methodology and how scripts are written and organised
- have patience to write and rewrite all your books into actionable content which should be around 100 pages.

Here are the tips to help you get started.

- **Read about screenplay and how it is written**

If you have not written a script before and you are convinced that it is something that you can do, I will advise not to jump into doing that. First of all, take time to learn about how scripts are written, how they are formatted, the screenplay software on the market and indeed, everything about scriptwriting. This will help you to do it in the right manner and properly. You don't have to rush over this. There is the tendency to think that you can learn about scriptwriting from the comfort of your home just after few hours of reading. No! Screenplay writing is an art and science that may take you months to learn how to do it. Remember that people spend years in colleges and universities to study how to write actionable scripts. So, if you are not ready to devote your time in learning about how to do it properly and all its aspects, it is better you don't start at all.

- **Learn from experts**

After reading books and theories on how to write a script, you need to study practical applications of all that you have read. The best way to see how the principles and ideas contained on the pages of books you have read are applied is to study scripts written by experts. Find successful screenplays and see how their writers organise their storyline and flashback. Take note of the ways the writers introduce characters and scenes or how they keep the audience in suspense or put them under tension before something negative or positive happens. You should also take note of their formatting style. If you study a couple screenplays keenly, you will be able to learn the nitty-gritty of screenplay writing and also how its basic principles are actually applied in reality. After going through this painful channel, you are ready to start creating a script from your book.

Creating a list of the essentials

- The setting of the story (environments where the scenes take place such as universities, bar, hotel, shops, church etc)
- The major characters of the entire movie
- Assign roles to each of the characters (protagonist and antagonist) and decide on how they come together or relate with each other
- What major things about each of the characters that you think your audience should know of
- The main conflict or core of the story, why and how it all begins
- The chief and most visual scenes in the book that have connection with the occurrence of the conflict
- Ten to twenty lines of your story that are vital to the story or upon which the story is built on
- The key overarching theme of the book

This list will serve as a guide to you. With it, you can start writing the script. But as I warned above, it has to be expertly done. If your script falls short of the required quality of a good screenplay, it will definitely not be considered by a producer and your effort will be an exercise in futility.

Important points to bear in mind when writing your scripts

Be mindful of the length: As I mentioned above, screenplay is different from a book. One of the major differences between them is that there is always a limit to the number of pages you can write in a screenplay. Many inexperience scriptwriters do not consider page limit when writing their scripts. The page range for a screenplay should be around 90-109 pages. You should make a conscientious effort to keep the number of your pages within this limit. The reason for this is because each page of the script is considered to be a minute of the screen-time. So, if you have a screenplay of 100 pages, it simply means that the film will last for 100 minutes which is an hour plus forty minutes. A movie of such duration is not short. On the other hand, if your script is shorter than the required number of pages, it simply means that the screentime will be shorter.

Make your point with few words: When turning your book into a screenplay, you should try to cover much of the scenes contained in the book, especially the major ones, but as briefly as possible. Brevity is a virtue that you should pursue in script writing. Describe scenes and tell your stories with few words but ensure that you transmit the core message and information it is meant for. Don't try to include all scenes and portion in your book in the script. A lot in your novel will be removed during the process of adapting it to script. You have to reduce or minimise the characters and subplots in your book expertly. This means that the cutting should not be carried out anyhow or in such a manner that the core message of the novel will be lost.

There are things that you should not include in your script. First bear in mind that you're a scriptwriter and not a producer or a director. So, your main role is to turn your book into an actionable script. Consequently, you should concentrate on that. Don't include camera notes, music or song notes and similar aspects. These are not your function, as you are not directing. It is the director of the movie that provides such cues on the pages where they are required.

Keep to the required structure and format: Scriptwriting is an art and science and as such, it has a structure and format that should be followed. It is quite different from other forms of literary works that have no formula. This is why I mentioned earlier that you should make out time to learn the structure and format or how to write a script and keep to the acceptable formula. Don't try to create your script according to your own structure. You risk wasting your time and energy if you don't abide by the right format and structure. Remember, always check scripts written by professionals. Evaluate your own script in the light of the screenplay of these skilful and professional scriptwriters. This will help you to determine the quality of your work.

Purchase quality screenwriting software: Nowadays, with improvements in software development technology, there are now different kinds of software which can be used to accomplish specific tasks. There are also some that are designed for scriptwriting. Whether you are very good or not, it will be good that you purchase quality screenwriter software. It is a good investment of money. Using it will make the task easier and will also make your work look more professional. A lot of such software are available on the market today. However, quality ones can be expensive. You may have to spend about $200 in order to purchase a good one. Take time to learn about scriptwriter software to learn the best ones on the market. Movie Magic Screenwriter and Final Draft are good examples of quality screenplay software.

Visualise all scenes when writing: As I have mentioned above, what is being acted is the script. This is why it is written with actionable language.

When you are writing the script, you should bear that in mind. Always think visually. You should not be a story teller when writing your script. Instead, your script should make your character to do something.

Don't forget to register your script when you are done: When you are through with the writing of your script, it is essential that you register it with a professional body like the Writers' Guild of America. Though this may cost you a small amount of money, it's worth doing as it will help you to draw the attention of the industry stakeholders to your book and also to protect your rights. Check the website of the organisation http://www.wga.org/members/membership-information/benefits to see what you will gain by becoming a member of this association. The next thing you should do after registering the book is to look for ways of attracting the attention of the top players in the industry.

Note that the above discussions are just about the right steps to follow to help you get started. It does not exhaust the list of all you should do and learn. There is indeed a lot to learn on the art of scriptwriting.

Hiring a screenplay writer

When it is not an option for you to do the script by yourself, the only option left for you is to hire a talented and professional scriptwriter. If you register with freelancer.com, guru.com, upwork.com or any freelancing site, you are going to find the right talent to handle the project for you. However, make sure that you hire the right person. There are a lot of professional scriptwriters out there. A lot of them have their own websites. Search for them on the Internet. But bear in mind that they do not render the same quality of services. Some are better than others in many aspects. So, if you want to hire a professional script writer, look for the best. Good scriptwriters possess certain qualities for which they are known. When you are hiring a scriptwriter, it is also of crucial importance that you learn these qualities and look out for a screenplay writer that possesses the qualities or at least 80 percent of these qualities. Before explaining these qualities, let me first enumerate the job specification or scope of scriptwriter.

Job scope of a scriptwriter

Whether you have a book from which the storyline will be drawn or not, there is always a limit to what a scriptwriter can do for you. But at the same time, the scriptwriters' work is not limited to the actual writing of the screenplay. Idea generation, research, plotting, character development, creation of the dialogues and the development of an engaging storyline are all within the job scope of a scriptwriter. Doing this creditably well may require them to carry out thorough research about a particular occupation or location that will be included in the screenplay. It is also their duty to revise scripts based on the guidelines provided by the director or a producer of a movie. So, when you are hiring a scriptwriter, it is good that you know how much the person can do for you.

Below are the qualities or skills a good screenplay writer should have and which you should look out for in a person that you will hire.

- **Creativity in writing**

A good scriptwriter should be a talented writer with a high level of creativity. He or she should be able to build a good and compelling plot, which movie production companies find attractive.

- **Ability to carry out interviews and research**

As mention above, the job description of a scriptwriter may require the person to carry out research and conduct interviews. So, a good scriptwriter should be able to conduct interviews. Interviews require good communication skills. A person who does not have good communication skill will not be able to interview people.

- **Persistence and determination**

Persistence and determination are important virtues which good scriptwriters should have. As I mentioned above, scriptwriting a project is not something that you can complete within a couple of days. It may take months or even more than a year to get a script written. It involves writing and rewriting until a finished work is produced. A person who easily gives up or who loses patience easily cannot be a scriptwriter. So, when you want to hire your scriptwriter, make sure that you hire a person that will have the patience to go through the stressful process of scriptwriting from beginning to end.

- **Hire a movie enthusiast**

Scriptwriting is a profession. However, such a profession can only be carried out effectively by a person that has a love of movies. Movies are nothing but scripts acted, filmed and shown to the audience. Any scriptwriter that has no passion for the movie industry will not know what the audience wants and will also lack the patience to start and complete such a time-consuming project.

- **Look for a story lover**

Storytelling is an essential aspect of scriptwriting. Any person who does not know how to tell a story will not be able to write a script. You may have already told your story in your book, but your scriptwriter is going to retell it in an actionable language. So, it is also crucial that the person has an interest in storytelling.

- **Good command of the language the script is being written in**

Just like a book writer, a screenplay writer is required to have a good command of the language you want your script to be in. You don't want a script with grammatical errors and wrong spellings. Often, people confuse good command of the language with the use of high sounding and sophisticated words. A writer shows his or her mastery of a language by his or her wealth of vocabulary of the language of use. But this does not mean using complicated words. Clarity and absence of ambiguity are good aspects of well written scripts. Scriptwriters are therefore required to aim at clarity of thoughts and language. The use of correct grammar is also a must. If your book is written in a language that is not the same as the language you want the script to be written in, it is of crucial importance that you hire a scriptwriter that has a thorough grasp of the language in which the book is written in even if you have a translated copy. Remember that translators are regarded as traitors, as they can give a different meaning to what an author actually wrote.

- **Hire a person that is conversant with multiple styles**

There are various styles, principles and theories of scriptwriting. It will be to your advantage to hire a writer that has good knowledge of the various styles of scriptwriting. He or she should also show the willingness to experiment with various styles on the same script so as to determine the most suitable style.

Other qualities required of a scriptwriter are as follows:

- A good scriptwriter should be able to work under pressure
- He or she should be disciplined.
- Scriptwriters are required to have good observational skills.
- He or she should be tolerant of criticisms.
- Scriptwriters should be able to sit for hours to write a script.
- Docility and ability to learn quickly or follow instructions are also good qualities of good scriptwriters.

The cost of hiring a scriptwriter

When you are hiring a scriptwriter, you should bear in mind that the scriptwriter will devote hours to your project. It is not a type of project that can be rushed or completed within a few hours. If you hire a scriptwriter, you are going to engage him or her for a long period of time. So, you should expect to pay a large amount of money for such a service. It does not matter whether you are going to pay per hour or a fixed amount. With regard to the cost, there is no stipulated amount that writers charge. Each scriptwriter charges a unique amount for their services. But you should expect to pay up to $4,000. The price can be more or less depending on the service provider. A professional scriptwriter can charge up to $30,000 to $50,000 or more. So, don't expect to pay a thousand dollars.

How much time does a scriptwriter require to complete the project?

You have seen the job description of screenplay writers. It is a tedious task. In your own case, you have a book already. This means that the script writer you hire will have to go through the book first to know what it is all about before crafting the storyline, scenes and the various aspects. Your writer will not be working alone. You also will be working with him or her. After reading your books and taking notes, he or she will create the beat sheet, which is also known as the punch-up. This sheet contains the major points of the plots. It will be forwarded to you for approval. If you are happy with the one-sided sheet, you will give a go-ahead order for the writer to continue and produce a draft of your screenplay. You can see that the number of days it will take to complete a script is also determined by you and not just by the writer. Supposing that you delay in going through and approving the beat-sheet, the scriptwriter will require more days to make up for the wasted time. There are other factors that can affect the delivery time. If your book is voluminous, the writer will also require more days to go through the books and take the necessary notes. So, when fixing deadlines, you should be realistic about it. It can take months or years to write a script. There are some scriptwriting projects that may take writers several years to complete.

Precautions to take when hiring a scriptwriter

There are some precautions that you should take when you are hiring a scriptwriter to ensure that nothing goes wrong on your side. Take note of these points.

Make sure that you hire a writer that can write a complete lengthy film script and not just somebody that will run out of ideas after completing a few pages. Request for samples from the writer you want to hire. Also go through his or her reviews to see what other clients they have worked for have to say about their services.

Secure your right over your script meaning that you have to ensure that you reap from the fruit of your labour and not another person taking what belongs to you. You can decide to hire a ghost-writer. In this case, the writer is not credited. You pay him or her an agreed amount and that is the end of his or her job. Alternatively, you can establish a credit situation in which the writer receives royalties if the film is eventually produced. The advantage of this option is that you will not be the person to pay the royalty if the writer has a credit. But the writer's name will appear in the movie as the screenplay writer. The book from where the story is drawn will also be indicated. Under this arrangement, the screenplay writer will be given two percent of the production budget and three percent of the producer's gross. This option also increases the possibility of your book getting turned into a movie. Some of the credited scriptwriters have agents and financiers that scrutinise and correct their works and ensure that screenplays are optioned and greenlighted.

Before beginning any project with a scriptwriter, it is also advisable that you get the scriptwriter to sign a confidentiality agreement. Many people may think this kind of agreement can be useless because a number of legal cases on this ended in an unsavoury manner for authors. However, it can also help, as there are a lot of people out there that have a conscience and can keep to agreements. Besides, for any book-to-movie-service, there is always one or more agreement to sign at a particular point. It should call for concern if your service provider does not present any agreement or contract to you.

Note that it can be more expensive to hire a ghost-writer than when you create a situation where the writer is credited. This is because they are not going to receive any possible royalties from the work.

Avoid rushing and managing the process. Give your scriptwriter enough time and freedom to complete this task for you. Bear in mind that they have been in the business of writing scripts for movie and so, they know how to go about it. If they have any need for any information or clarification, they will get in contact with you.

Assessing the quality of the script

There is a feeling of happiness and joy that comes when your scriptwriter has finished and submitted the final draft to you or you have finished writing your script. But don't immediately start looking for solicitation. It is good that you hand it over to a third person to go through it, edit and assess it. It is in this way that you will be able to get an unbiased evaluation of your work and industry opinion of the feasibility of the project. There are a number of script assessment professionals that can offer you such a service. The cost of this service can be somewhat high as it also involves long hours of work. Some script editors and assessment service providers charge a fixed price while some charge per week. It can take an average of one week for a screenplay of about 90 to 100 pages to be read through, assessed and edited. You may be charged about $2000 to $3000 for this service if the editor goes through the work in a week. You can get the service at a less or more expensive rate.

How to Get Your Screenplay Solicited

Now, you have written your screenplay. But film producers need to know about it and read through it to see if they can produce it into movie. How do you get the producers to ask for your screenplay? It is a common myth that producers do not receive or consider unsolicited scripts. It all depends on your location and the producers involved. For example, in the US, movie producers do not accept unsolicited scripts for legal reasons. But in Australia, there are some that accept it. However, in the business world, the normal thing is for a producer to solicit for your script or ask you to bring an agent. However, this does not mean that you cannot contact producers or send a query letter to them directly. Indeed, many beginners do contact producers and send their script to them but in the end, they will not get any reply from them. It all depends on your approach. You should understand a good number of film producing companies ignore unsolicited submissions. First, they don't want to enter into any legal battle with any person that will come up to claim that their ideas have been stolen and turned into movies. Secondly, they receive lots of emails from scriptwriters. They do not have time to read through them.

However, you can still get a company to solicit for your script. One error that a lot of new writers make is to send their script and synopsis as an attachment to a filmmaking industry the first time they are contacting them. According to Cate Baum, "this is the last way to get seen." The best approach to this according to Richard Walter, a professional scriptwriter, is to send an email (query letter) to a producer inquiring if your script can be accepted. If the company wants to take a look at it, they will surely reply and ask you to send it over. In this case, it is no longer an unsolicited script.

If you eventually got solicited, you should also be professional when sending your script. Just write a letter of about three lines that summarises your script and then email it with your script attached to it. You can also send the script via post. You don't have to include your bios and your photos as some people do. Avoid asking them to sign a confidentiality agreement before they can read your script. It is too early to ask for such a deal. If you request for that, they are likely to commit your script to the bin.

Besides the above, entering film festival script competitions is a good means of improving your chances of getting the attention of producers and agents. But you can only utilise this option if you have a script already. Secondly, you need to spend some money in order to participate in a script competition. However, if you succeed in going far into the competition or if you emerge the overall winner, you will get your money back, as your effort will be rewarded monetary prizes or other suitable forms of awards. Potential buyers also attend these festivals in search of great work or talented scriptwriters. So, you are likely to get the attention of a buyer if you have good work. A typical example of script competition is the UK Film Festival Script Competitions, Los Angeles Film Festival, Nantucket Film Festival, Arundel Festival Theatre Trail, Congleton Playwriting Competition, Northern Writers' Awards, Australian Writers' Resource Competitions and many more.

Is It Right to Follow Up Your Submission?

There is no need following up your submission. In the first place, a producer may accept a script today and it may take them up to a year or more to go through it and take a decision on that. So, you need to exercise patience. Besides, if a film producing company likes your script, they will definitely contact you either via email or phone or any other suitable means. Bear in mind that they have a lot of emails to read. So, wait patiently for their reply. If they don't reply, take it as you see it. Forget about the project. However, there are situations where you can follow up your submission. If a producer gives a timeframe within which you should get a reply after soliciting for your script, you can send a follow-up note at the expiration of the timeframe.

A good script will definitely get green lighted and if you have one, you are most likely going to make it into a movie. There are two important elements that your script should have to get approval from producers. The first one is originality. Your storyline should be original and unique. Nobody wants to enter into any legal battle with any person. High concept books also are easily accepted by producers. High concept scripts are screenplays with a simple but poignant tale to tell. The second element that will make a book get easily accepted is the audience it appeals to. It is important to have a script that appeals to four important audiences and they are men, women, young people under the age of 25 years and elderly ones (pensioners). A script that appeals to these four audiences is often called a four quadrant. Typical examples of such movies are *Indiana Jones*, *Meet The Parents*, *Mrs. Doubtfire* and *Titanic*. Visit https://screencraft.org/2013/11/22/four-quadrant-film-10-essential-elements/ to know more about the characteristic features of such a script.

Other things that will help your script be accepted by producers are as follows:
- Ensure that your book has good Amazon editorial reviews.
- Make sure that your book is well written, organised and presented.
- Work hard to grow your online and offline fan base. Try to achieve popularity on social media, Google search Goodreads and others.
- Try selling a lot of your books.

However, bear in mind that some producers do not consider all these factors when they are assessing scripts. They make their decisions based on the work before them.

Pitching: An Important Aspect of a Query Letter

As I mentioned above, the best way to get your script solicited is to send a letter or an email to a producing company telling them about your script and asking if they will be interested in it. This letter is what is called a query letter. I have already talked about what you should include in the letter. But I would like to discuss one important aspect of the letter, the part where you give a brief description of your script. This is called pitching. Pitching is the art of explaining the core or main idea of your script to a producer, studio executive or an agent. It summarises the script putting emphasis on the major characters, conflict and genre. It can be done either in writing or verbally. The length depends on whether it is done verbally or in writing. In writing, the length can range from one page to six page pitch; but if it is done verbally, it can be about 15 to 20 minutes verbal description. There are a lot of books on pitching. You can also find informative articles on pitching on the Internet. Workshops are also organised on pitching. Read articles and attend workshops on that in order to learn the various approaches to pitching. There are also consultants that offer professional advice on it.

Some of these approaches may be contradictory but their objectives are the same, which is getting a producer to be interested in your script. So, gather as much information as you can and learn various approaches and use the one that best suits your style. Mastering the art of pitching can be somewhat challenging but you cannot run away from it. You need to be perfect with the art before you approach an agent or a producer.

As I mentioned earlier, there are a lot of resources on pitching on the Internet. You can also find a number of books written on it in local libraries. Just type into the search box of your preferred search engines the combinations of the following: pitching, pitching to a studio, film, movie, screen writing and competition. The search result will bring up various websites that provide information, tips, advice and guidelines on pitching.

Optioning Your Screenplay

There are situations where a producer, an investor or a director may be interested in your script but they are not sure if they will produce the film or not and they want to secure the exclusive first-pick rights on it in case they decide to make the film. This is called an option. The main objective of an option is to stop the scriptwriter from giving the script to another producer, director or agent within a stipulated period of time.

Option does not give any financial benefit, as the amount for it is very small. A script can be optioned with $200. It is even possible for a script to be optioned with a dollar or $0. However, it helps to boost the ego of the scriptwriter. It is a good thing that some producer is captivated by your script. But bear in mind that the fact a script is optioned does not mean that it will be made into a movie. It is simply carried out to stop you from showing it to another company within a specified period.

Film producing companies go into option because they want to look into the script within the stipulated timeframe to see if it is something that they will make into a movie. There are some movie makers that option a script as a strategy of preventing the script from being acted because it is quite similar with another script they want to produce. Such an option is really very bad as it stops you from actually realising your dream of adapting your book into a movie.

When negotiating option, you should bear these points into consideration and don't think that something great is happening or that your movie will soon be produced. A good way to ensure that a producer does not keep your script out of the market is to negotiate a short period option. In this way, you will not miss out on other opportunities that are likely to come your way. Option period should not be over two years. So, an option period of a year to two is ok.

Take note of the clauses that are attached to the option. You need to have an expert evaluate your option contract before you sign it. There are some producers that include clauses in the option that will prevent the scriptwriter from marketing and promoting their book as a means of making sure that your story does not become widely known pending when they produce the movie. Therefore, don't accept any option that will not allow you to promote your book or sell it to a publisher so that your chances of adapting your book into a movie do not depend entirely on the company that options your script. You can see why it is very crucial that you learn the business aspects of filmmaking. If you have a good mastery of the business as well as the legal aspects of movie making, you will know when a producer is trying to take undue advantage of your work.

If you are afraid of optioning your script, you can also sell it to an interested producer or agent. It is advisable that you hire an agent to help you with the process and to negotiate favourable terms for you to ensure that you are not cheated. Below are three important parts of option that you should handle with caution.

Note that any kind of books or literary works such as short stories, magazine articles, novels, fiction and nonfiction books can be unpublished work. It is advisable that you have a published work before looking for an option opportunity, as the print imprimatur will negotiate for the highest option price.

Note that the studio or buyer that eventually exercises the option does not purchase all rights. There are some rights that are exclusively for the scriptwriter unless the contract says otherwise. So, when negotiating option, you should reserve the book rights, radio rights, live stage rights and eBook format rights as well as the sequel, prequel and character rights. Depending on your reputation in the industry, you may also reserve extra rights for yourself.

Does selling of certain rights to a studio conflict with the rights of the publisher?

Publishers also purchase certain rights such as rights to all print and electronic verbamtim book rights, audio for verbatim rights, merchandise, serial, abridgements, and subsidiary rights. Many new writers have problem with this when comes to knowing which rights to reserve to the publisher. This should not be any problem. If you are confused about which of these rights to reserve for the publisher, then you have to hire an agent. A reliable and intelligent agent knows which rights to leave for the publisher. An entertainment attorney can also be of help to you, as they know the industry requirements in this regard.

Does a film production company require a manuscript before making an offer?

No! Manuscripts are not necessarily required. It all depends on a company making an offer. Some will demand for them while there are some that do not require a manuscript before making an offer. But you should bear in mind that the purchase price for rights over a book or a manuscript is quite different from the amount paid for a screenplay.

You can sell rights to unpublished manuscripts but it is normally sold at a low price. You can also sell unsuccessful books or books that are selling at a moderate rate. If the book is not very popular or is modestly successful, you will still be able to sell the rights, but at an amount within the region of $50,000 (more or less). Another factor that will determine the cost is whether it is your first sale or not. For your first sale, expect around $300,000 to $600,000. It is also possible to sell a screenplay for a price that's around or even above $1million.

The option payment

As I have already mentioned above, the option payment is usually small. But it is not static. It can vary. You have to negotiate a fair amount based on a number of factors such as the potential budget of the film and your track record. Some experts are of the opinion that the option payment should be up to 10% of the purchase price of the script. The truth is that the amount can be negotiated. It is left for you to negotiate a fair amount. There are options payments that were negotiated at a low amount of about $200 and some that were negotiated for $50,000. Further, there are some producers that will want you to sign an option contract that pays a dollar or nothing. This is not a good contract. Any company that really has interest in your script will definitely offer a good price for it. Besides, if they pay nothing to get you sign the option agreement, there is no guarantee that they will be able to finance the purchase of the script.

The option period

I have also explained the option period and what you should be a guide. Suffice it to mention that at the expiration of the period, you can also renegotiate the option especially if there is a clause for extension. Note that if the producer is not able to pay for the film at the expiration of the option period, you will keep back the option payment and all the rights to the script will come back to you.

The Purchase Price

The purchase price of the script refers to the amount of money a producing company or an agent will eventually pay the scriptwriter for the screenplay if they eventually decide to turn it into movie. It is normally called the exercise price. It can be regarded as an offset of the option upfront payment (the initial amount paid for the option). Again, there is no fixed amount for the purchase price. It is also negotiable. But normally, it is calculated as a percentage of the budget for the film. Some experts suggest

10% of the total budget for the movie. Take this amount as the balance of what is left after the option payment has been made. So, when negotiating, you should consider what has already been paid to you and negotiate an amount that when added to it will be equal to the purchase price of the movie. In this way, you are not cheated. You should also consider your reputation as a writer as well as the quality of your script when negotiating.

Don't forget these!

I have suggested above that you hire an agent or somebody that is conversant with the industry to negotiate for you. Producers also want to get the best terms and put you at a disadvantaged position. Some contracts may omit certain essentials to the detriment of the scriptwriter. One important fee that you should always be on the lookout for is the non-applicable fee. If there is an option for renewal of the contract, it is advisable that you request for a non-applicable renewal amount. With this, you will not lose on the exercise price.

When negotiating your option, ensure that the contract gives you the screenwriting credit. Many producers normally don't grant this request, especially if they edit the script. But according to the WGA credit rules, a scriptwriter is given the screenwriting credit if at least 33% of a produced screenplay is written by him or her. This means that no matter how much the producer edited your story, if 33% of the entire contents are written by you, you are entitled to a screen writing credit. So, when negotiating your option agreement, remember to negotiate for that.

To make this work without much problem, you should also negotiate for the right to do the first rewriting of your work. This is important because almost all screenplays submitted by writers are edited before they are acted. This aspect is particularly important to you if the producer is also hiring you for editing. But bear in mind if you are hired for rewriting, your work starts after the option period.

Don't forget to negotiate a favourable payment schedule in your contract. Many producers are not different from certain unscrupulous producers who pay their employees anything they like. When you are negotiating your contract, request that payment be made within 1-2 weeks from the time you submit all the deliverables. This favours you because if the producer decides not to produce your movie, you have already been paid and you will not be completely on the losing end. But if you allow the producer to pay as they like, it may be difficult to get paid if they eventually decide not to produce your movie again.

Also, don't forget to stipulate the payment method you prefer. It can be via bank check, direct deposit into your bank account, wire transfer, credit card payment or any other method. But make sure that you are comfortable with the payment method they are using. Also mention the currency you would like to be paid in.

As I mentioned above, be realistic in your negotiation. Always consider your experience and reputation during negotiation. The producers also take that into consideration. Don't expect to have as much favourable terms as another accomplished scriptwriter when you are optioning your first work. Regardless of how great your work is, you should not disregard the realities of the industry. Gradually, you will become popular in the industry if you are really a talented author or scriptwriter. This is the time you will begin to command respect. But this does not mean that you should settle for peanuts. Try to get the most favourable terms you can for yourself but be realistic with your terms.

Do I Need to Get Attachment for My Movie?

Before explaining what an attachment means in the movie industry, I want to state categorically that it is not the function of the screenplay writer (the principal writer) to provide any attachment. It is the duty of their agent or producer to do so. So, if any person asks you to provide an attachment, politely refer them to your agent or producer.

Attachment in the movie industry has a different meaning from its conventional meaning. In the movie industry, it refers to a person different from the writer that helps in the development of a screenplay for production but is hired during the production of the movie. Normally, the attachment can be a director, an actor or producer. It can also be a funder or any person that will help in the production of the movie. The reason why attachment is made is because the screenplay writer is not able to reach the right people.

There are a number of people that can serve as an attachment to a script. In some situations, it can be the lead action or a movie producer who has optioned the script. There is normally a formal agreement put in place in this type of agreement. Attachment can also come with no formal agreement. In this case, it is informal involving friends of the writer who assist him or her in promoting the script based on the understanding that the script can only be sold if the friend gets a paid role in the production of the movie. There is the third type of attachment, which is similar to the first type. Here, the scriptwriter submits the screenplay to a manager, agent or a producer who in turn includes himself or herself as attachment and sends it to a studio that will make the film. The scriptwriter may not be aware of this arrangement in this type of attachment. This kind of attachment may result in legal battles between the scriptwriter and the producer. This usually occurs when the scriptwriter discovers that the prospective buyer has received the script from the attachment included without his or her consent.

As a scriptwriter, you should be wary of attachment. If a producer wants to include themselves as an attachment so that they can show the script to a funder or a person that can make it, it is important that you have an agreement with the producer. Make sure that the terms of the agreement are favourable to you. Don't sign an agreement with unfavourable terms. Politely decline the offer and send a letter, an email or a fax message in respect of that to the prospective attachment explaining your reasons why you are rejecting the attachment. In this way, there will be no misunderstanding or possible legal battle in the future regarding that.

Take Note!

Once your script is optioned and sold, you have little or no part to play again in the making of the movie. The producer may request for your input or ask you to visit the set. But they are not obliged to do so.

I have mentioned it above but let me repeat it here again. Don't expect your script to be made into a movie as it is. The producing company has to make some edits, which may require the rewriting of the script without your contribution unless you are hired for the rewriting.

Lastly, I will advise you to get an entertainment lawyer to help you assess any deal before you sign it. In this way, you will avoid signing something that will put you into a difficult legal position.

Note that you can option your book and save yourself the stress of putting it into a script unless you negotiate to have an input. However, if you option your book, the producer is at freedom to decide who will write the script for them. In case you are hired to do the script, you have no right over the script as it becomes a work-for-hire in this situation. This means that you are working like an employee. In other words, it is more advantageous to option a script because you receive payment for the rights and also for the script. You will also get royalties as the author of the script if your screenplay gets the green light. A second advantage you will get if you write your script is that the content will be your story and not just what another scriptwriter thinks. Sometimes, screenplay writers give a different interpretation of the stories and scenes to what the author has in mind.

Though this can happen during the rewrite but the writer rewriting the original script sees your own thoughts and interpretation of your work.

Also bear in mind that screenplays can be sold outright rather than optioning it. This method has some economic advantage over option. You will not be dealing with middlemen or the people that will option the rights. You will be transacting directly with the industry players. However, you will still need a manager or an agent to help with the sale negotiation. A script can be sold for $300 to $600,000 depending on the quality and your negotiation power. If the sale pulls through, you are going to give about 10 percent to your agent or manager who can also be your producer. If your producer is acting as your agent, the entire commission will still come back to you when the movie is made insofar as you negotiated and included this in your agreement with him.

If the sale is not successful, don't give up. Take a look at it again, repackage it and give it a trial again. Sometimes, scripts are sold after a second or even a third attempt. Some don't give up if the first attempt fails.

Production

Once a studio accepts your script and decides to make the movie, they will make all necessary arrangement for the production before rolling the camera. They will have to source for the right talents (the actors), source for funds for execution of the projects and obtain all necessary rights. It is also their responsibility to define the audience and the target market. In other words, you have nothing much to contribute. Your part ends as an author with the selling of your book or the screenplay, unless you negotiate to make an input during the shooting or in any other area.

The approval to make a movie is known as green light in the film industry. If you get a green light for your script, the purchase price will be paid to you. As I have mentioned above, there is no fixed amount for this. It is based on what you are able to negotiate. But in most cases, it can be within the range of 2 – 3 percent or more of the production budget plus a cap. So, if the budget for the production of a movie is $5million and you negotiate 2 percent of the budget and cap of $225,000, you will receive $100,000 plus $225,000 as your purchase price. The cap amount is fixed but the percentage amount depends on the budget. If your book or script is being turned into a series, you will make more money as you will be paid for each episode. Apart from these payments, you are also going to receive royalties for your work.

Royalty and Reselling Rights

Rights are crucial issues in the movie industry. Many writers and authors are complaining that producers and film studios are cheating them and not giving them adequate compensation for using their intellectual properties (scripts and books are considered as intellectual properties and are therefore copyrighted). The producers and studios on the other hand are also complaining that authors are greedy and would like to make too much gain after selling their rights. Writers and authors want to know what their rights are, whether they will receive royalty for their script and whether they can resell their script after it has been made the first time or after a period of time.

In the first instance, royalty in the movie industry is known as residual. According to an entertainment attorney, Jonathan Handel, the rights of an author of a script turned into movie depend on the contract they have with the producer and/or whether the transaction is carried in compliance with the Writers Guild laws (this is if the parties involved are signatories to the Writer Guild agreement). As a matter of fact, the producer is obliged to pay the writer all that is stipulated in the contract. If your contract stipulates that you are paid a certain percentage of net profit or stipulated proceeds, then you are to receive that at least theoretically. This amount is normally 5%. But it can be more or less depending on what you are able to negotiate. If the deal is contracted under the laws of Writers Guild, the author is supposed to receive a residual once the movie is made and is put in any other media like DVD for home video, television and new media. However, according to Writers Guild Association requirements, writers are not paid any residual for the theatrical release of the movie.

Once the video is made the first time, you have no right again to resell it. Original scripts prepared under a WGA law are excluded here. The writer of such a script has additional rights, which may be applied under the complex concept of separated rights.

Why are writers entitled to residuals?

Books and scripts are intellectual property and as such their authors hold the copyright. Consequently, all derivative works like movies to be made from their works come under their control. The creative rights of authors also prevent producers or any other person from manipulating their works. These rights of authors constitute serious obstacles to studios and film producers that would like to make films from these works.

These obstacles necessitate the need for the producers and authors to arrive at a compromise in a deal where the authors give up their authorship rights to the producers/studios and receive certain benefits including residuals in an exchange. You can say, it is fair enough for authors to receive residuals.

Note that all participants or people involved in the production of a movie are given residuals as they are not royalties and not bonuses. Gaffers, for example, don't receive residuals.

Creating a Book into a TV Series

The process of creating a book into a TV series is quite similar with the process of creating a book into a movie which I have discussed extensively above. But there are also some differences in it. Here, not intending to repeat what has been said above, I am going to explain the process of turning a book into a TV series.

The first point that I have to make here is that creating a TV series is not as expensive as creating a movie. It is also less time consuming when compared with movie production. The screenplay writing and pitching of TV series are almost the same with those of film production. But each becomes distinct after this stage. When a work is green lighted, it has to be outlined as a means of refining it so that it will turn into a pilot script. This normally occurs during the fall period. The author may be required to provide a story document after the studio has accepted to produce and air it. Note that pitching is normally done between June and September and by fall, the scripts that scaled through are refined in outlines during the fall season.

The next stage after the refining of the scripts that passed the pitching is the preparation of the pilot scripts, which is also known as pilot episode, television pilot or tele-movie. It is a standalone episode normally ordered by a TV network to determine how successful a series will be. It is a test episode of a large TV movie. They are prototypes that prepare the ground for the actual series. The tele-movie is normally the first episode of a series that is transmitted to the public as an introduction to the rest of the series. However, before they are aired to the public, they must sell a series. It will help the TV networks to judge whether the cost of producing the series is worth it. The pilot is followed in the production of the remaining series.

You can do the pilot script or hire a writer to do it for you. Once it is viewed and necessary corrections made by the studio or network, you will edit and rewrite the draft to reflect the corrections made. This normally is done before the Christmas holiday begins. It is important that you revise the network draft before the month of January.

The next stage is the casting of the script. Unfortunately, not every script gets to this stage. So, you should count yourself blessed and lucky if you are able to get to this stage. TV networks order either series or pilots. If they place a direct-to-series order, they will need to hire writers to create the next scripts after pilots.

Actors are required for the casting and filming of each of the episodes of the TV series. As a writer, you have nothing much to contribute at this stage unless you have a contract to be involved in the casting and filming. Normally, when a TV network approves a pilot, they will hire a showrunner and producers. The showrunner takes charge of everything now using the script to direct the casting and filming of the show, overseeing all aspects of the movie till the end. The showrunner works in collaboration with the producer in hiring the members of the crew including the director, assistant producer, scriptwriters and any other talents required for the project.

The filming and production of the show normally takes place during the months of March and April. You can see how long it takes for a script to be turned into a TV series. After the filming and production, there are other offices that handle the post production tasks. The editing of sounds and correction of colors are carried out in the post production facilities.

When every post production work has been concluded, the TV network will start what is known as upfront which is the presentation of the show to the advertisers around the second and third week of May. If you are lucky, your show will get advertisers that will sponsor it. Once advertisers show interest, all discussions and deals will be contracted. The entire process of making a TV series can be grouped into three, namely, preproduction, production and postproduction.

Storyrocket: A Useful Resource for Writers and Scriptwriters

As I mentioned above, there are a lot of resources in the industry today. I have discussed some but I would like to single out storyrocket in this chapter as I consider it a very useful resource for authors, screenplay writers and directors as well as producers. It is a platform where you show your work as a writer. You can also find other authors' works that have been adapted into movie on this site. It covers a wide range of literary and movie genres. So, regardless of the type of book you have, you can display it on the site.

Storyrocket connects writers and film producers as well as film directors. If you create an account in the site for free, you will be assigned your own mini-site where you can upload your pitch, main character description, logline, tagline, photos, elevator pitch, video trailer, synopsis and every important aspect of your work that you will want a producer to see. You can share your pitch package on the social media anytime you like. Producers also register with the site to search for pitch package that interest them.

The site management understands the risk posting contents to the public poses for writers. Thus, they have taken necessary measures to ensure that writers are not cheated. So, when you post your work on the site, only 5 pages are seen by producers searching for content. So, if any producer is interested in your work and would like to see more, the person has to contact you. In other words, storyrocket does not interfere in any manner in any deal you have with your prospective producer. You have total control of the deal.

If you succeed in getting a deal with a producer, regardless of the amount involved, the site has no share in it. Users of their services pay a monthly fee, the amount of which depends on the monthly plan they are into. But the lowest amount is $8.33 per month for 10 projects. Registering with the site does not attract any long time commitment. Visit the site https://www.storyrocket.com/ to learn about it and the various services they offer users. You can also check this site http://www.imdb.com/. It is similar to https://www.storyrocket.com/.

SECTION THREE: THE LEGAL STUFF

Turning your book into a film is much more than writing the scripts, optioning it or selling it outright and getting all the necessary payments. It has its legal aspects, which should be properly handled from the onset to avoid unnecessary legal battles in the future. Many authors have instituted court cases against some producers or studios who they thought took undue advantage of them. Some of these cases were judged in favour of the producers. If you don't want to engage in any lawsuit with any person, it is essential that you take time to learn about the legal aspects of film making, register your work and get legal guidance from an experienced legal firm that specialises in handling cases related to intellectual properties and movie industries. In this section, I am going to discuss the legal aspects of film production, especially the copyright aspects and what are protected by it.

Disclaimer: I am not a lawyer. You must check all legalities printed in this book yourself. All countries can vary re copyright laws and any other laws. This is not legal advice. I recommend to obtain an attorney for legal advice.

Chapter 5: Copyright Protection Law

As mentioned above, scripts and books are intellectual properties and are protected by the copyright law, which forbids any person from using another person's intellectual property without express permission from the owner. Despite the existence of such laws, there are still copyright infringements here and there. Sometimes, clear cases of copyright infringements are decided by the court in favour of the thief simply because the owner did not do what's needed on time or because he or she has little knowledge of what is protected or how to protect it. In this chapter, I am going to discuss copyright, what is protected by copyright law and how to protect a script or a book. This chapter also provides insight on how you can handle copyright issues.

Overview of the Copyright

Copyright is the legal term for the right given to an originator, owner of, author of or assignee of an intellectual property such as a script or a book to print, perform, film, record literary, artistic or musical material and to authorise others to do the same. This right is an alienable right and it is recognised internationally and in all jurisdictions, even though there may be nuances in its applications under various jurisdiction. The principle behind the law is always the same everywhere, which is to help owners of intellectual properties to benefit from the fruits of their labours and to prevent others from stealing their works. Scriptwriters and authors as briefly shown above have the exclusive rights to:

- authorise other people to use their work
- adapt their works into a form they like
- produce derivative works from it
- to sell, lease and transfer ownership of their work to another person
- display their works publicly.

The copyright law also does not allow any person to change, alter or modify copyrighted materials without express permission from their owners. Copyright law does not allow any person to produce works that have similar characters and plots with copyrighted materials. Consequently, film producers and studios must obtain express permission, valid transfer or assignment before they can use copyright materials. If they fail to obtain such permissions, they will be in for a court case for copyright infringement.

As mentioned above, copyright law is globally accepted but its application differs from country to country. In some countries like the United States of America, there are systems of registering copyright ownership as well as accepted legal means of transferring or assigning the same. In Australia for example, there is no agency in charge of copyright registration because there is no system for such registration. The registration is completely free and automatic without requiring you to make any publication or public notice. Works come under the protection of copyright from the moment they are written and recorded in some way. However, if you are living in such a jurisdiction, it is a good practice that you inscribe a copyright notice on your book or script. But for scriptwriters and authors in the United States of America, it is a different ball game. The country has an office and a system for the registration of works for their authors to have copyright protection.

The United States Copyright Office has a website www.copyright.gov which maintains a database of all copyrighted work. Before any script or book is copyrighted by the office, they normally run a search of their database. The service attracts some fees, unless you do the search by yourself. The registration process is very simple. Just visit www.copyright.gov/forms/ and fill out the Form CO online; make a payment of $3 and you are done. The process today does not require any public notice in accordance with the Berne Convention. However, if you make a notice of copyright, it can give you some advantage.

Such a notice provides some information about the author and the first publication date of the work. It is also a veritable means of announcing to the public that a work is about to be copyrighted by the owner of the copyright. Some experts advise authors to register their works in various countries or jurisdiction. However, copyrighting a work does not mean that your claim is 100% accurate and cannot be challenged in a court but at least, it gives you leverage should such a case arise in the future.

In France, there is a system for copyright registration also. The office of the public registry of film and broadcasting which is under the control of the Centre Nationale du Cinema et de l'Image Animee (CNC) handles the registration. However, whether a work is registered or not, it has the protection of copyright right from the time it is created. You can check www.cnc.rca.fr to obtain more information about the system and how it works.

Nowadays, there are non-governmental organisations and guilds that offer screenplay registration services. Typical examples of such institutions are Writers Guild of America, East (WGAE, www.wgaeast.org), Writers Copyright Association UK (www.wcauk.com) and Writers Guild of America, West (WGAW: www.wgaeast.org). In France, the SACD in Paris performs the same functions as the Writers Guild of America. International bodies are today providing International Standard Identification Numbers (ISAN) for audiovisual works. These numbers help to identify unique works internationally. They are inscribed in works in a non-visual manner. They are referred to as watermark. Though, with them, it will be easy to recognise a work but they are not proof ownership and they give no information about the copyright owners.

Given the importance of copyright laws, insurance providers normally require studios and film producers to provide the following documents:

- Copyright report/clearance report/clearance opinion
- Title report/opinion
- Written rights agreements and releases
- Confirmation of rights to source materials

There are other checks that may be carried out by producers and studios to ensure that they are not guilty of copyright infringement. However, don't think that these producers and studios are angels and will not in any way try to cheat you. A good number of them are looking for loopholes from your side so that they will take undue advantage of that and rip you off.

What Is Protected By Copyright Law

It is important that you copyright your books and scripts, especially if there is a system for that in your jurisdiction. But unfortunately, and against the wish of many writers, copyright law does not protect everything. There are limitations to what can be protected by copyright. It is good that you know the extent of protection you have under copyright law. This is important because sometimes writers believe that they have been cheated while in actual fact nobody cheated them.

The first point that I have to make here is that copyright protects only the author's expression which includes the writers' voice, approach to the material and their manner of telling their stories. Put differently, copyright law offers no protection to concepts, themes and story ideas, rather it protects only building up, embellishment or ingredients used in expressing the ideas. The implication of this is that other writers as well as producers do not violate any copyright law by borrowing ideas and other materials not protected by copyright law. But they are in for prosecution if they borrow author's expressions.

However, it is always a challenging task to determine when an idea is sufficiently expressed for the author to be given the credit of that copyright. If an idea is not sufficiently expressed, it makes no sense to claim the ownership. In this regard, a synopsis of a page may not be considered an idea while a script of a 20-pages may be considered so. There are a number of court cases that proved this to be right and showed the difficulty involved in owning copyright of insufficiently expressed ideas. Sheldon vs. Metro-Goldwyn Pictures Corp., and Musto vs. Meyer court cases throw more light on this. Read more about them here http://www.scriptmag.com/features/legal-protecting-your-writing.

However, the fact that an idea is not protected by copyright law does not mean that it cannot be protected as it is also regarded as a type of intellectual property. The question to be answered now is: how does one protect their ideas?

The answer is simple. When negotiating a contract, it is important that you bear in mind that the terms of the contract is your legal support. So, it is essential that you take everything into consideration. Try to negotiate a contract that will oblige a producer to pay for your intellectual ideas if they use it. If a producer accepts and signs such a contract, then they are obliged to pay you for your ideas in accordance with the stipulations of the contract. In other words, having an enforceable contract is a veritable means of protecting an idea.

Contracts are of two types, namely, oral and written contracts. Contrary to the thinking of some people, oral contracts can be enforceable depending on whether or not they are considered valid and binding in your jurisdiction. If it is taken to be legally binding and valid in your jurisdiction, I will advise you to always go for a written contract because of the difficulty involved in proving the terms of an agreement contracted orally.

Also, bear in mind that what is not covered by copyright, which are regarded as some forms of intellectual properties, may be protected by other forms of intellectual property laws such as patent law. For example, processes, ideas, methods, procedures and the likes are not covered by copyright but the patent law protects them. In a similar manner, with trademark law, you can protect names, slogans, titles and symbols.

If you are still not sure of whether your work is protected by copyright or not, you can contact an experienced lawyer who specialises in handling cases related to intellectual properties and the likes.

Protecting Your Book/Screenplay

I believe that by now you should know a little bit or at least a lay man's understanding of copyright, what it protects and the complexity involved in determining what constitute an expression of ideas. The movie industries have thieves in them. Your script can be stolen or abused once you submit it for option. Given this, you should go the extra mile in protecting your ideas and work. There are certain things that you can do in order to offer stronger protection to your script and works.

It is advisable that you register your work with the writers' guild in your country or any similar organisation or guild that will ensure that your script is not stolen. When you register your work with a guild, you have established the identity of the work as well as the date of the completion of the work. With the registration, you have established a proof of priority of ownership. On the contrary, it will be difficult or impossible to prove your ownership of a script if you send it to an agent or producer before registering it. The duration of the protection offered to your idea depends on the institution or guild offering it. For example, the Writers Guild of America offers a 10 years protection to registered script. Note that registration with any of these institutions will not give you more protection than what the law gives to authors or owners of intellectual property. Apart from scripts, there are these nongovernment institutions that register outlines, treatments and synopses.

In summary, once you complete your script, make sure that you register it before handing it over to an agent or a producer. If you hire a scriptwriter to adapt your book into a script for you, it is also important that you register your book and have the writer sign a work-for-hire agreement. If you have no contract with a script writer, it is also possible for the writer to steal the idea from your book and create a script for themselves and sell it. The writer can also decline your offer after you have explained your ideas to him or her and then use for themselves. So, be very careful with such a project.

What to Do When Your Right Is Infringed On

If you're a victim of copyright infringement, there is nothing much you can do other than to go to court and seek for compensation. But as I mentioned above, copyright cases are sometimes difficult to judge. Sometimes, the judgement can even be against the victim. So, if you think that you are a victim of copyright infringement, you should look for a strong lawyer with the required experience and expertise to handle such cases to argue for the enforcement of your right by the court. Your lawyer should access all facts of the case to ascertain whether your right has been infringed upon and the possibility of obtaining justice in the court. There is no point going to court or doing a trial and error court case if in actual fact, your intellectual property is not stolen or violated in anyway. Your attorney should be in a better position to advice you based on the facts of the case.

You can also take a step further by reporting the case to the appropriate authorities that handles cases of violation of intellectual properties. For example, in the US, the Federal Bureau of Investigation has a section that looks into such cases. They can sue the culprit and initiate a criminal prosecution charges against the person. Depending on the severity of the case, the offender may forfeit all revenues made from the work and all will be returned to you.

Another good means of handling copyright infringement is to contact the thief directly. Some people are normally willing to settle copyright infringement in a friendly manner. But it will be good that you hire a lawyer to negotiate on your behalf so that you will get a favourable term in the negotiation. Don't settle for something that you will regret afterwards. If they are giving you favourable terms, it makes no sense going to court, as you are not sure whether you will win or lose. Good cases have been lost on technical issues as well as on other matters. Legal battle, in my opinion, should be the last resort to the issue.

Regardless of the action you will take, it is of crucial importance that you first discover the person that stole your idea. In this way, you will be dealing with the wrong person.

Who Owns the Copyright: Producer Or the Author?

I have already said a lot above that answered the question that formed the subheading being discussed now. Copyright ownership does not have a straightforward answer. It all depends on the circumstances that surround the creation of the work. In the literary and movie industries, books and scripts are owned by the original persons that copyrighted it. In the movie industry per se, the owner of a film is the principal producer and director except in a situation where the works are created by the employees. As I have mentioned above, scriptwriters and authors can sell their copyright or ownership of their work in exchange for money including the residual that they will be paid if the movie is made in other forms.

Note that if a book has two authors, both authors have the ownership of the book. However, there are exceptions to this. In a situation where each author contributed to a distinct portion of the book, each person has ownership of the part they created. If ownership belongs to two people, one of them cannot adapt the work without express permission of the other. Both of them should come to terms or reach an agreement before a script or a movie can be made from the work unless one has already transferred their ownership.

Difference between Authorship and Ownership of Copyright

There is a subtle difference between authorship and ownership. They are very similar but in the copyright law, there are not actually the same. The two terms mean exactly what they sound like. Authorship goes to the person that creates or writes a book or script while the ownership goes to the person that has the copyright or legal rights over the work. Ownership based on the above has almost the same meaning with copyright.

There are situations where a person can be the author and the owner of a script at the same time. It is also possible for the author and owner of a work to be two different people. If I write a book for myself, I am both the author and the owner. But if I write it for another person or at the instance of another person and get remunerated after completing the project, I am not the author but not the owner of the work.

There is a third situation where the person that writes the book or the script is neither the author nor the owner. This is normally the situation in work-for-hire contract. In this situation, you are hired to write a script or a book for a person. You get all you're due at the completion of the work. The person that hires you will be the owner of the book and its author. This is also the situation in an employer-and-employee relationship. If you are an employee of a company and writing of a book for your employers becomes part of your job, the authorship and ownership of any book you write as part of your work for the business that hired you belongs to your employer unless it is stipulated otherwise in your contract agreement with your employer. As always, it is the terms and conditions in your contract that will guide your relationship with your master. It is important that you understand the differences between these two words, as they are important words in the industry. They are together with copyright, trademark, patent and the likes the bases of most of the court cases in the film industry. This is why I am taking time to explain them and the difference between them.

Chapter 6: Obstacles to Avoid

The movie industry has impressive prospects for the talented individuals but it is one that you should approach with caution and carefulness. The industry has saints and sinners as well. If you fall into the hands of a saint, you will laugh but the reverse will be the case if you enter a deal with a dubious person. Some individuals as well as businesses in the industry are looking for people to take advantage of. There are some bottlenecks and pitfalls to avoid in order not to enter into any trouble or court cases with any person. In this chapter, I will be exposing some of the pitfalls that you should really avoid.

Identifying and Dealing with all Right Transaction Pitfalls

I have explained copyright, authorship and ownership above. These rights are very important in the industry. Most of the court cases that occur in the industry revolve around these terms as they have to do with rights. One of the main reasons why many people encounter these problems relating to rights is because they did not take time to learn about them from the onset or they were ignorant of them thinking that it will not occur. So, if you have any plan to adapt your book into a movie or to sell your script, it is essential that you learn about these rights and how to handle any transaction in the industry that involves right. Even if you have an agent, you don't have to presume that they know everything or can handle everything. Yes, they can handle you deal but always find out how they are handling issues on rights. In this way, it will be less unlikely for them to miss out on any important details regarding rights.

Get All the Rights from the Real Owners

If you are using any person's material or intellectual property when preparing a script, ensure that you obtain permission from the person or you acquire the right to use the material unless it is a clear case of "borrowing ideas." If you are not sure whether what you borrow is an idea or expression of the author, you have to contact your lawyer for a discussion on that.

I have taken time to explain copyright in the chapter above. I don't have to repeat what I have said earlier. But bear in mind that it is not only producers and studios that steal another person's work. Authors and script writers also do that in a number of ways. For example, it may be a case of copyright infringement to write a script based on an already produced movie unless it is established that what is borrowed is an idea and not expression of an idea. You can go to jail for such an act. So, don't use any person's expression of ideas without getting the rights from the person. If you co-author a book with another person, abide by what has been said about that if you want to adapt the book into a movie.

Know the Rights that Are Included in the Deal

Many people, especially new comers in the industry, easily get confused about rights. This is why I suggest that you learn about it so that you will not get confused. If you have a deal to turn a book into a movie, you should strictly abide by what is stipulated in your license or contract. Don't go beyond that. For example, a license to turn a script into a movie is not the same as a license to turn the same book in a TV show, a sequel, novelisation or any other thing. You're limited by your license or contract. Anything outside that may be a case of rights infringement. So, obtain right for all that you intend to do.

Keep to Your Obligation to Avoid the Loss of Your Rights

This is almost repeating what has been said above in a more forceful and different way. Know what is in your contract agreement and abide by that. It is no news today to hear that a studio or an individual forfeited a huge amount of money running in millions to another person simply because rights were abused either intentionally or unintentionally. So, make an effort not to be a victim of such occurrence. Apart from obligation on the use of another person's intellectual property, there may be other requirements that you should abide by, depending on your locality. For example, governments of certain places require their citizens to submit all scripts to them for approval. So, if you are residing in such a society where such copyright rules are obtainable, don't fail to submit your script for approval before selling it or submitting it for option. In this way, you will be able to avoid any problem.

Be Mindful of Characters

Just like books and scripts, characters in books and films are copyrighted and trademarked and thus cannot be used without the express permission of their originator. This does not mean that you can use a character in another script in your work but what is copyrighted and trademarked is the role played by the character. Put differently, you can use a character in another writer's script in the same way the originator of the character uses it. If you do, you may be in for a serious legal battle with the originator of the character. But you can use the same character and depict him or her in a different manner.

Getting Educated about the Movie Industry

If you are entering into the movie industry, it is a grave mistake on your side not to get educated about the industry. I have mentioned this point before but let me repeat it in another way. This is because knowledge is power and it is very essential for any scriptwriter and indeed any one to have it. In this regard, I deem it important to tell you some of the important sources of information or sources where you can learn a great deal about the movie industry.

To begin with, there is a good deal of information about the cinema industry today. Seminars and workshops are organised here and there in various places in the cinema industry. You should make it a point of duty to attend some of these conferences at least occasionally. You should also purchase and read books like this one as they will enlighten you more about the industry. There are also magazines and daily trade papers in the movie industry. Reading these dailies are a veritable means of becoming au courant with the happenings in the industry. Three prominent dailies in the industry are The Hollywood Reporter and Variety for the US market and Screen International for international related topics. Ecran Total and Le Film Français are the two popular ones in France.

The Internet is a good source of information. Many institutions and organisations in the industry have their websites stuffed with useful contents. Some of the websites to visit in order to obtain useful information on the industry are:
www.imdb.com
www.lefilmfrancais.com
www.screendaily.com
www.deadline.com

Bulletin boards, magazines and newsletters are as follows:

- Encore Magazine: http://mumbrella.com.au/category/encore-news

- Australian Film Television and Radio School (AFTRS): www.aftrs.edu.au/e-bulletin

- AFTRS OPEN Short Course Update for NSW short courses: www.aftrs.edu.au/short-courses

- Filmnet: http://filmnet.yuku.com

Note: at the time of printing, all the websites were working. As the Internet changes rapidly, some sites might no longer be live when you read this book. That is, of course, out of our control.

Chapter 7: Bonus

Note: at the time of printing, all the websites below were working. As the internet changes rapidly, some sites might no longer be live when you read this book. That is, of course, out of our control.

Are There Directories For Books Made Into Movies?

Yes! You will find a lot of directories in the Internet that provide lists of books adapted and made into movies. URL of some of these directories are:

- http://www.listchallenges.com/best-books-made-into-movies

- http://www.paperbackswap.com/Books-Made-Movies/tag/8969/

- http://harborview.ccsdschools.com/directory/special_area/elizabeth_parker__mlis/chldren_s_books_made_into_movies

- https://www.npr.org/sections/monkeysee/2011/03/02/134029161/your-2011-books-into-films-lineup-from-eyre-to-water-to-desert

You can search for more on the Internet using any of your preferred search engines such as Google Chrome, Internet Explorer, Mozilla Firefox and others.

Are There Directories For Film Producers Of Specific Genres?

Yes! You will also find a lot of directories online with rich information about film producers. Here are some of the links to some of these Internet directories for film producers:

- https://www.hollywoodreporter.com/lists/30-powerful-film-producers-hollywood-883194/item/michael-bay-brad-fuller-andrew-883173

- http://www.writewords.org.uk/directory/level1_pages.asp?typeid=57

- http://www.filmcontact.com/directory

- http://www.boogar.com/resources/mediabroadcast/movie_production.htm

What Are the Consequences of Adapting My Book Into a Movie Or TV Series?

Adapting your book into a movie or TV series has both positive and negative consequences. On the positive, it is a veritable means of marketing and promoting your book. Movie enthusiasts and other people who have not heard of your movie will come to know about it when they watch the movie. This is likely to increase the number of copies you will sell as it increases the probability that many of them will look for the book if they like the movie. A typical example of an author that sold many copies of her book after a movie made from it was released is Vikas Swarup, the author of the book *Q&A*. She sold only 35,000 in three years before the *Slumdog Millionaire*, the movie version of the book was introduced in the market. Within the first two months of the release of the movie, additional 35,000 copies of the book were sold. This definitely increased her revenue from her book.

Turning your book into a movie also multiplies the income you generate from your intellectual property. If your book gets solicited, you will get free money for the option. If it gets green lighted, your earning will increase as well. It can even change your life depending on the movie budget and what comes out of the movie as you will also be paid royalties for other derivative works. You will not be surprised to know that J.K. Rowling, the author of Harry Potter became not just the richest author in history but also the second richest woman in the entertainment industry thanks to the royalty she receives from the adaptation of book. Imagined how much she has made if she were paid 5% of $4.4billion revenue generated from sales of all Harry Porter movies as residual for her effort. The author of the Lord of the Rings J.R.R is another author that made a lot of money from the movie adaptation of the book. The film alone earned $2.9 billion.

On the negative side, your book or script can be stolen. Once you submit your book or script for option, you are vulnerable to theft and all kinds of abuse. As I mentioned above, the book can be altered and modified such that it may be quite different from what you have in mind. Other script writers and editors that will work on it can give it a different interpretation.

There is also the danger of the producer coming out with inferior production that will give a negative view on the main book or movie that has no resemblance to the original book. This was the experience of Ursula K. Le Guin, an acclaimed and experienced author. The adaptation of her book *Earthsea Series* does not resemble the original work.

What Are Things You Should Not Bore Yourself With

There are certain aspects of the entire project that you should not bother yourself about no matter your skills. They are better handled by the producer's experts. Don't worry your head about the following:

- Writing the songs or soundtrack for the movie that will be made from your book
- Recording the soundtrack
- Establishing a budget for the production of the movie
- Making the movie poster
- Establishing the character studies or illustrations
- Listing the possible directors of the movies
- Contacting actors, bands or any other person that will be involved in the production of the movie

You may be wondering why I said you should not bore yourself with all these. The reason is quite simple, any person or company that accepts to produce your story will handle all these aspects. You can see that doing these activities will amount to an exercise in futility or a complete waste of time.

Copyright and Trademarks: This publication is Copyrighted 2018 by Zoodoo Publishing. All products, publications, software and services mentioned and recommended in this publication are protected by trademarks. In such instance, all trademarks & copyright belong to the respective owners. All rights reserved. No part of this book may be reproduced or transferred in any form or by any means, graphic, electronic, or mechanical, including photocopying, recording, taping, or by any information storage retrieval system, without the written permission of the authors. Pictures used in this book are either royalty free pictures bought from stock-photo websites or have the source mentioned underneath the picture.

Disclaimer and Legal Notice: This product is not legal or medical advice and should not be interpreted in that manner. You need to do your own due-diligence to determine if the content of this product is right for you. The author and the affiliates of this product are not liable for any damages or losses associated with the content in this product. While every attempt has been made to verify the information shared in this publication, neither the author nor the affiliates assume any responsibility for errors, omissions or contrary interpretation of the subject matter herein. Any perceived slights to any specific person(s) or organization(s) are purely unintentional. We have no control over the nature, content and availability of the web sites listed in this book. The inclusion of any web site links does not necessarily imply a recommendation or endorse the views expressed within them. Zoodoo Publishing takes no responsibility for, and will not be liable for, the websites being temporarily unavailable or being removed from the Internet. The accuracy and completeness of information provided herein and opinions stated herein are not guaranteed or warranted to produce any particular results, and the advice and strategies, contained herein may not be suitable for every individual. The author shall not be liable for any loss incurred as a consequence of the use and application, directly or indirectly, of any information presented in this work. This publication is designed to provide information in regards to the subject matter covered. The information included in this book has been compiled to give an overview of the subject s and detail some of the symptoms, treatments etc. that are available to people with this condition. It is not intended to give medical advice. For a firm diagnosis of your condition, and for a treatment plan suitable for you, you should consult your doctor or consultant. The writer of this book and the publisher are not responsible for any damages or negative consequences following any of the treatments or methods highlighted in this book. Website links are for informational purposes and should not be seen as a personal endorsement; the same applies to the products detailed in this book. The reader should also be aware that although the web links included were correct at the time of writing, they may become out of date in the future.

www.ingramcontent.com/pod-product-compliance
Lightning Source LLC
Chambersburg PA
CBHW071722040426
42446CB00011B/2175